A RECIPE FOR REWIRING YOUR BRAIN, FINDING YOUR *fun* AND REDISCOVERING *you* AGAIN!

EAT PLAY love

AMANDA EVANS

Eat PLAY Love: A Recipe for Rewiring Your Brain, Finding Your FUN & Rediscovering YOU Again!

YGTMedia Co. Press Trade Paperback Edition

Published in Canada, for Global Distribution by YGTMedia Co.

www.ygtmedia.co/publishing

ISBN trade paperback: 978-1-989716-51-9

eBook: 978-1-989716-52-6

To order additional copies of this book: publishing@ygtmedia.co

Developmental Editing by Tania Jane Moraes-Vaz

Edited by Kelly Lamb and Christine Stock

Book design by Doris Chung

Cover design by Michelle Fairbanks

Author Photos by Kirsten Schollig

Printed in North America

To all who have ever felt unseen:
this book is for you.

Table of Contents

Prologue

A LETTER TO THE READER

Dear Reader,

Thank you for allowing me into your space and into your journey. I want you to know that you are not alone. I've been where you are now.

I've been on a similar path as you, and I understand your pain, your disappointment, your fears, and your worries because I've felt them. You see, nearly ten years ago, on a random Tuesday in June, my life changed in an instant. I was in a car accident that left me with a brain injury and set me on quite a healing journey.

I'm here to help you on your own healing journey by sharing my story with love, compassion, realness, and openness. I remember feeling deeply alone and often misunderstood. Having a label or invisible illness can create that. This is why I felt called to write this book.

I don't want someone going through their own healing journey to feel as alone and unheard as I did. So, if you currently feel that way, I hope you feel seen and heard here.

I remember this one moment when I heard someone share their journey of hope and healing. It sparked a new sense of belief and hope in what could be. For me, there were a lot of fears that I might not get better or beyond the me with all the symptoms and challenges that came along with a brain injury. I heard a video where a mom talked about her son who had a brain injury.

She spoke about how their new goal became to put 110 percent into his healing journey and "show people what's possible." That really hit home, and in that moment, I made that promise to myself. But before I could show another what was possible, I knew I had to show myself. So, I put 110 percent of me into my healing and found my own way home through it all.

This journey reminded me that when we have an awakening, a huge healing journey, or an experience that defies the odds, that reminds us that miracles really do happen and that we truly are never stuck, we have to show up and *show people what's possible*. Each story reminds us.

I also know that I read MANY books and watched many videos like this to get the healing "ahas" and experiences I did. It felt like brain injuries never had one that spoke to the heart and the super sensitive person navigating this journey. It took many different books, programs, teachers, and healers to help me understand all the things that supported me and understand the why behind this. Writing this is a guide that is meant to align you with all those "ahas," tools, and takeaways all in one book as opposed to needing to find and read them all!

I hope it brings you whatever you are in need of; and in the meantime, here is a little more before you begin!

Before you start reading, I want to take some time to ground your experience. To help you feel guided. To help you cultivate trust in yourself while you're navigating this book and your own personal journey.

This letter is a reminder that you *can* trust yourself . . . even if your way of reading or learning is neurodivergent—different to how another person may navigate a book, life, or learning experience.

And that is actually why I wrote the book: so you, who feels like your brain is different, can feel whole. Because you are! Don't let anyone, including your own mind, tell you otherwise.

I want to ensure that you don't feel overwhelmed when this book is hitting you where it might be hurting. I remember reading being a challenge in itself during my recovery, so I want to make it as easy to read and navigate as can be. You can read it any way that aligns for you, in the way that makes it feel applicable, relatable, doable, and transferable to you, your life, and your journey.

Before we start, I want to talk about what to do if you feel stuck or overwhelmed. Knowing firsthand how brain injuries and trauma can make the nervous system, brain, and body feel overwhelmed, this is where I want to begin.

Breathe. Be gentle. Love yourself here. That's what to do if you get stuck or feel overwhelmed. Ask yourself: "What do I need?"

And then listen for the next step.

For example: You sit down and can feel a massive headache coming on, yet you want to continue reading. This makes you feel confused and leaves you wondering, *Do I read this now or not?*

When that happens, I invite you to pause, BREATHE deep breaths, and say: "What do I personally need *at this* moment?"

Listen to what your body is trying to tell you. Listen to your heart. Perhaps the answer comes in and says something like: "Go play, don't read right now" or "Take a break and meditate" or "Go bake a cake." The answer could be: "Sit down and read Chapter 7; it has the answer my brain, body, heart, and soul have been asking for. It is what I need; there is something here to be explored, which is why my head hurts."

Trust yourself while trusting that the book has got you. Your team of healers, helpers, and loved ones have got you. And your heart and self-healing abilities have got you.

Know that you get to hear the truth about what you need in every moment, that you have the tools you need, and that *how you read this book* happens in a way and timeline that truly honors you. If you get stuck and don't feel like taking the next step, ask yourself why.

Is it resistance? Are you perhaps unsure whether this book will truly help you (because you feel like nothing has)? If so, I get you, and I'm encouraging you to notice it and keep going. Notice this resistance, then get back to the steps and the book.

Is it your needing space to live, to play, to integrate the steps? If so, take the advice I share to go "stay and play" and not be so serious for a change. And remember, where you are right now IS enough . . . so trust the step that you are in (and also know that this will all make more sense soon!).

So HOW do you do it?

This might sound silly. You may be thinking, *We start at the beginning and keep reading until we get to the end.* (Like how we are taught to read a book in school.)

Here's the thing: That is a great way to read this book! But not the only way.

Start where you are. Start at the beginning of the book. But after that, you can choose. Honor that a chapter may or may not resonate.

There may be a chapter that needs your attention or feels challenging. There may be one that has so many aha moments that you need to read it multiple times. It's up to you, and it's okay! Our brains and bodies love repetition, so I strongly encourage you to come back to what supports you time and time again.

If you want to go to a certain chapter because it seems to resonate with you, go for it. If you need to reread certain sections over again, there's no judgment. I want to make it as easy to read and navigate as can be.

If you've been struggling to communicate certain feelings with your friends or family members, feel free to flag passages or chapters for them. Or maybe just pass along the whole darn book. This is meant to help you!

You can take as long as you need to on a specific chapter (of the book and in your life). "Turtle rules" rule! Why? Because slow is steady, it isn't bad. Having a brain injury slowed me down big time! But something big can happen in the SLOW. You can let go of being who the world needs you to be and honor who you want to be.

You don't need to speed up to another person's pace. You can listen to your needs and take as much time as necessary. Or if you start to become aware of your needs and realize you need to skip ahead to a particular chapter because it's speaking to you at the moment, do it! If you start to feel so energized, inspired, and aligned that you want to speed up, go for it! I celebrate that too.

You are grounding in a new experience, you are rewiring your brain, and you are finding more FUN, all while changing your life at the root.

I respect you knowing your personal needs, finding your own groove, and discovering the support that helps you. When you have read this book in full, you get to choose which ingredients you infuse into *your* recipe of life. You get to choose which ingredients support you. The recipe is yours to create. You get to choose!

Find the chapters and build your own "recipe book." That way, you can come back to it at any time. Reread, retry, realign, and rewire—all while finding your fun and reminding yourself of WHO YOU ARE and how you choose to live, love, and PLAY your way.

Remember: This is your life, this is your awakening, this is your healing, and this is your story. You get to choose every single thing.

So always, in all ways, do what honors you, the unique you that was, the *you* that is, and the *you* who IS becoming more of who you truly are.

That said, there are some things we need to talk about. This isn't your typical "read me" and "do as I say and follow the steps exactly as I share them" kind of book. That doesn't fly in my world!

This is a book that SHOWS and SHARES and lets you show up for your journey. Think kindergarten "show and share" style, like when a kid comes and shows you their favorite stuffed animal and it reminds you of yours and how that makes you feel. This book is like that, and just as you remember your stuffed animal, you will learn that my shares will show you something of yours and how to show up *new* within it all. As you. With your specific lessons, soul curriculum, inner knowings, and heart-led and healing aha moments.

This is your opportunity to finally find your MAGIC, make meaning of all the mess, of all the mud, and find your way to your FUN and your fulfilled you (even if right now all you can think about wanting is to "go back to who you were," "feel normal," "fit in," and finally be able to show up at regular social events without feeling quite so alone or misunderstood).

There is nothing that I have shared that I haven't lived. But I also haven't lived your story and don't want you to feel like you need to do life my way. **I want you to find your way, while having mine as a way to help you build your guidebook.** This is my "show and share" journey that will hopefully help you.

To honor this "show and share" approach, I share "The Band-Aid Story."

Because this is kind of how the book will go. I share a little, then let you take what resonates and apply it to your personal journey. This story is one I learned about in teacher's college that felt deeply applicable to the journey of navigating life with an invisible illness or "disability" (something I refer to as exceptionalities or sensitive superpowers).

Because in truth, these are our sensitive superpowers, even when society may not always see them, label them, or understand them that way.

This story is about what you need. Finding your tools is not about what works for another, it is simply about what does align for you. What you need might be very different from what I need.

THE BAND-AID STORY AND HOW IT RELATES TO YOUR READING AND HEALING JOURNEY

You've probably had a lot of doctors try to slap a "Band-Aid" fix on your symptoms, your label, or your health and happiness challenges. Well, this book is different. It's not a one-size-fits-all approach to healing. It's here to help you heal at the level your heart is ready for, to help find the root rather than to put a Band-Aid on you and call it a day.

I write in the "show and share" format because that's the way we make our own meaning and find our takeaways from listening and reflecting, so we can then take action on the aha moments. What's fair isn't giving every person the same thing, the same solution, or the same fix. Fair is giving everyone what they actually need.

Your needs aren't seen. And sometimes symptoms mask your ability to express, identify, and confidently and coherently share those needs. How often has someone looked at you in disbelief that you aren't feeling well because you look good to them? They don't see your invisible illness, but it's there. They don't realize that the person you used to be isn't the one you are now. Believe me, I get it! I had many people look at me perplexed and say, "But you look good!"

For example, let's imagine there are four people in a doctor's office. The first person has a cut on their finger, and the doctor gives them a Band-Aid. That makes sense.

The second person has a broken leg. They, too, are given a Band-Aid because everybody needs one to be fair. Does it make sense? Not so much.

The third person has a migraine and is very anxious because it feels hard to communicate and stay present, which then creates a whole other loop of fear and shame of being misunderstood. They are given a Band-Aid. Fair? Well . . . yes, but helpful? No.

The fourth person has a concussion (brain injury). They have a myriad of symptoms, and their doctor says, "Here's the Band-Aid."

Clearly, treating every illness in the same way doesn't help. A generic treatment doesn't support someone who has a challenge that requires a more tailored one. Yet some systems for healing almost take a cookie-cutter approach to each illness. It's great if the Band-Aid works for some, but it's not the solution or "soul"-ution for everyone.

You, like me, may require something more than treating individual symptoms as they appear. You may want to get to the root and truly heal by applying love to places that are hurting. You may have sensitive superpowers, a nervous system that has been over-taxed, some perfectionistic tendencies, and unexpressed emotions that are wanting to be tended to during this healing journey.

A Band-Aid can only do so much.

I suggest that you only listen to what honors you and advocate for what you need based on your knowledge of yourself. The need may also be met by seeking support outside the medical field in a way that meets your sensitive superpowers and body in the way it requires, which may also be in a holistic way (understanding that some symptoms have a deeper meaning). They may be pointing to what's underneath the symptom, the problem, or the label to get at the root—to get the soul healing alongside the healing of the body and the mind.

The company I started when I came to the other side of this journey is called "Mind Body Soul Miracles," and I say this to remind you that this book takes a perspective that supports the healing of invisible disabilities/illnesses/labels with an approach that encompasses all three: your body, your soul, and your mind.

My story is not your story. My solutions (or "soul"-utions) may not be yours. But they also might be. My sharing may inform some aspects of your mind, body, and soul to align in a way that helps you receive the healing.

Healing is often a return to wholeness, and my intention is that your mind, body, and soul are whole and work together to give you what you desire and need. So, remember this when or if you are in a moment of wondering how to navigate what is coming up for you.

This book is a call for you to come home to who you were always meant to be. Your pain, your symptoms, your needs are all valid. They matter. You matter. You are not "too much" or "too (whatever label you've been given)." You are whole as you are. All you need is love, deep breaths, and tools that honor you on your healing "**journey**." And that looks and feels different for every single one of us.

I learned so much on my journey to healing, to finding myself, and I want to share my story and my knowledge with you. I want to help you on your journey.

Thank you for coming along for this ride. I'm so glad you're here.

Love,

Amanda

Chapter 1

THE LOTUS

Maybe the journey isn't about becoming anything. Maybe the journey is about unbecoming everything that wasn't you in the first place, so you can be the person you were meant to be.

–Paulo Coelho

If you picked up this book, I'm guessing that you are well on your way through some kind of "**journey**." And no, I don't mean the band Journey that sings the song "Don't Stop Believin'," because likely, you stopped believing a long time ago. You may even be thinking, *What does she mean by journey . . . this freaking SUCKS!*

Chances are you're reading this because you have some type of invisible illness, have experienced trauma or a traumatic brain injury and are feeling pretty "stuck." Stuck in your symptoms, stuck in your trauma, stuck in feeling like you're not being heard or seen or helped. First, I hear you, I see you, and oh boy, do I get you!

I have a feeling that you haven't felt truly heard, seen, or understood in a long time. So, I need you to know how much I truly mean this: you are not alone. All of you—even the parts that feel the most *broken*—fit right here. All of *who you are* is welcome here.

After my accident, so many things became overwhelming. What used to be a regular action or routine experience was now a challenge with my brain injury, and I felt like I was stuck in the mud, unable to move forward or concentrate for any length of time. If that's where you're at, please be gentle with yourself.

When it comes to something like health journeys, the band Journey does have a point in their chart-topping song. Believing and cultivating self-trust is the most important step on the healing journey. Let me give you an example. Let's say you want to bake a cake. Before you start the baking process, you have to believe that you will a) find every ingredient you need to bake the cake you desire, and b) if you are unable to find every ingredient, you have to trust yourself enough to be resourceful and adapt the recipe as needed. You have to believe that you can bake that cake before you can actually take the steps to create it. If you don't believe in your ability to do so, then you'll never be able to have your cake (and eat it too). Pun intended!

Self-belief is key. You can have all the ingredients right in front of you, but if your self-belief is lacking or broken, baking a cake will feel like you've been asked to climb your own personal Mount Everest. In order to go first and do anything your heart desires, you have to first believe.

Then take each ingredient (or life circumstance), mix them together (adapt, figure out what works for you), put it all in the oven (reflect and trust that you've done everything you can), and BAM, you have a cake (your desired outcome). Then you get to decorate the cake, eat it, enjoy it, and share all the love that is this *cake* (and maybe even dance around while you eat it too!).

Now, chances are that you haven't eaten CAKE in a long time. You are likely on a bunch of protocols—special diets for your gut or strict rules for eating (and living)—and feel like it's hard to socialize, let alone celebrate! So, if the cake and partying are out, you perhaps believe that your dreams and the life you truly want are out as well.

Let's start there. Because all of that matters. You matter, and your dreams matter too. This feeling is all too familiar to me because it's exactly the place I found myself at once upon a time: out of "cake," out of dreams, and definitely out of faith and FUN.

I remember feeling like every day was hard. I had no desire or passion left in me. I dreaded waking up each day and doing it all over again. I was sick of "doing"—constantly doing everything for everyone else. Chasing after the applause, the perfection, the coveted "she's doing it all so well" validation from everyone else (and from myself). I was hardest on myself.

If you're anything like I was, you may be feeling pretty darn depressed, anxious, and tired with a capital T ("tired" being the understatement of the year). And it isn't your typical exhaustion after having a long day of doing whatever it is you're doing. No, it is the "I have no life left in me, and I don't know why I am not getting any better or why sleep doesn't help me feel more awake or *alive*" kind of tired.

If you're currently experiencing this feeling, know that it's a part of your journey, wherever that's leading you. For me, this was an awakening. It just took me a while to see it that way. And that's okay, as it's all part of the process. You have to feel it, heal it, and find your FUN (fun being a key ingredient)! Most of the time, fun is missing from the recipe, and I want to change that.

This book is about flipping the switch on healing from trauma and adding in the missing ingredients: EAT (whatever the **** you want), PLAY (because it gets to be playful and fun or else what is the point?!), and LOVE (love is the only way, for yourself and others)!

These are the ingredients we need more of when we're deep in the mud. But just like the lotus flower that blooms and rises through the murkiness, you, too, will bloom and thrive through it.

It may not feel like it right now. That's when we need someone holding space for us, to feel seen and to hear a story of possibility. That's why I am here. I'm going to share my lotus journey. My moment to rise. But much like the lotus flower, the rising did not come from a pretty place.

I was deep—like six feet deep—in the MUD. Stuck, sticky icky in the mud kind of stuck. Like the kind of mud that gets on your clothes, and no matter how many times you wash them or try to "fix" it, NOTHING WORKS! That kind of mud.

That's normally when we start referring to it as a "journey" because we start looking for the good in it, for the *silver lining*. Or as I call it, *the rainbows* amid the BIGGEST STORMS.

We start looking for the lotus amid the mud.

And if you are searching for your lotus amid the mud, perhaps you are experiencing something that has changed your life drastically. I remember when I finally got to the point in my recovery where I started referring to it as a healing *JOURNEY*. That was the moment when it became less of a *recovery* and more of an *unlearning* and *relearning*—when I started learning about who I *really* am, how to love and accept every part of myself, and how to find a way when it felt like there no longer was one.

Perhaps you're also six feet deep, stuck in your own mud. Maybe you, too, have tried everything to heal, to seek the answers outside of yourself rather than listening to the voice within. Maybe you have some sort of label, a diagnosis, or have had a life-changing event that has fundamentally changed who you are. Or maybe the same has happened to your child, and you feel helpless and don't know what to do next.

Initially, for me, it started out as just that—one label, one word, one diagnosis, one life-altering event—but it soon became my identity, the outfit I began to wear every single day. A signature look that everyone associated with me. Before long, it felt like me—the person, my likes and dislikes, my desires, my quirks—were forgotten. The label was all everyone saw.

Life as I knew it no longer felt the same. My whole life transformed from living to surviving—going from appointment to appointment, test to test, and trying one protocol, one doctor, one medication after another. I felt like I'd tried just about everything, from acupuncture to every medication under the sun to meeting with numerous specialists, psychologists, neuropsychologists, therapists, osteopaths, naturopaths, chiropractors (and even receiving Botox for migraines). Everyone I met with all tried to fix my condition, to treat my label and "manage" the many symptoms and cognitive issues.

Somewhere along the way, I felt like I stopped living—I felt like I lost me. My self. My soul.

That was my story, at least.

For me, the mud was a brain injury, and not even a "severe one," according to the doctors. I was diagnosed with a mild traumatic brain injury, like somehow including the word "mild" in the diagnosis made it okay. But there was nothing mild about it, and it was not okay. I was not okay.

Yet I tried to make it seem like I was fine. I smiled through the pain until I reached a point where I couldn't do it anymore. Being this version of me was no longer okay. Nor was it a place that I was willing to stay. That's when my journey began. I began peeling back the layers of the onion to get to the truth and find a way forward—my own way forward. To find the real me that was hidden and buried deep beneath all the things I thought were me.

I have since learned that accidents are never accidental. It turns out there was a part of me that was asking for more: more truth, more honesty, more time for me, more acceptance, more compassion, more love, and more fun. I realized that before my accident, I never knew how to ask for or fully receive these things—from others or myself. I was a version of myself who put everyone else's needs before my own, who had a powerful heart to love but was scared to be loved and to receive love (without feeling guilty or like I "should" be the one giving and holding space for others instead).

Perhaps these feelings resonate because you've been there, and maybe you still are. You might even think these are the most important qualities to have, the ones that actually make you a good person. I know I thought this way for as long as I can remember; I was wearing it as a badge of honor.

Maybe your accident is the Universe's way of calling you back to you, your self, so you can learn to ask for your needs and wants to be met, learn to receive, and learn to love all parts of yourself. Yes, even the ones that feel broken and unlovable.

Perhaps this is your chance to lean into and really discover who you are and what you are capable and truly worthy of!

You see, maybe that's the point of a journey. Maybe there is meaning in all the mess. **Maybe the breakdown is a runway for your biggest breakthrough, which will help you soar.**

Maybe, just maybe, there is something growing underneath all that mud. Perhaps this is life calling you to finally heal from the root. Like a lotus seed that is planted, and slowly, with the right nutrients, environment, and consistent nurture and care, it starts to bloom.

So, get comfy and cozy because it's about to get real. I will start by telling you about my mud. And then I want to hear and learn all about yours. (I'll show you mine if you show me yours!)

Chapter 2

THE MUD

June 5, 2012.

The exact date that everything changed.

Somehow, when something big happens, we always remember the date. It marks a moment in time. The moment when everything has changed forever. Though on the outside, everything will look and feel the same (in most cases), on the inside, everything has shifted. For you, for them, and everyone else. What's next is learning how to live in this "new normal," trying to reconcile the YOU that you used to be with the YOU that is on the other side of this.

I was twenty years old and in my second year of university where I was studying to be a teacher—something I had been dreaming about being since I was a little girl. This was my biggest dream, one that I never stopped believing in, and I would do ANYTHING to make it happen. That's when *it*—the life-changing moment—happened.

It was a summer morning, and I was frantically getting ready to go to a work training session with my sister. I was rushing and indecisive about how I wanted to do my hair. At the last minute, I threw it up in one of those plastic white hair clips and stuck my sunglasses on top of my head. I hopped in the front seat, playing the role of the passenger as I always did when my sister was driving, holding her tea in one hand and her smoothie in the other.

We were just starting on our way when **it** happened. The CRASH. The moment when everything in my life no longer felt the same, when I no longer felt the same.

All I remember about the crash is how that damn hair clip shattered upon impact . . . and the weird way time slowed down and sped up all at once.

On a quiet residential street where the speed limit was slow, we were in an accident. A car rear-ended us. We didn't see it coming. Although our car was totaled, there were no broken bones, and my sister and I seemed okay. At least we thought we were okay. Except, I wasn't. I didn't realize it in the moment, but my life as I knew it had suddenly changed. Me as the sociable, smart, fun-loving young woman on the cusp of her independent life no longer existed. She was gone, nowhere to be found. I became very slow and confused, and I was in a lot of pain.

Several of my symptoms started that day, yet at that time, I felt like I would be just fine. When I went to the doctor's office, I did an awful job of expressing what I was feeling, which in reality, was a very real symptom of a concussion. Naturally, I didn't get the support I needed because I wasn't able to accurately communicate how I was feeling.

I was frustrated and emotionally exhausted, and I minimized my pain because I didn't want to be negative. I'd always been a positive person and didn't want to start looking at the glass as half empty, even though it would have been totally valid.

Somewhere along the way, it became clear that my brain was not the same. My irritability, emotional outbursts, and cognitive issues were reflecting something deeper than a mere headache or ringing in my ears. Something happened to me the day of the accident. It was as if every part of my brain had been rearranged, and nothing made any sense. I didn't make any sense.

Yet my senses were heightened: I was sensitive to light, to noise, and to emotions (like big time!)—both my own and those of others. I remember that no one was allowed to use loud and angry voices around me because it hurt my brain too much. I didn't much mind that part, to be honest, but the sensitivity to people's emotions came with its own frustrations. It basically meant I was sensitive to people, and for a person who loved people and being around others, this felt like the worst thing that could happen.

Over the years, my sensitivity increased, and I became sensitive to foods, sensitive to smells, and just sensitive to everything. I was overwhelmed by very little stimulation.

When you experience trauma   traumatic brain injuries in particular— you are basically prescribed **rest**. You are told to slow down, to PAUSE, to lie in a dark room, and to not DO anything. Personally, I think this is the most challenging protocol because trying to rest when you're in that much pain and not being able to do the things you truly love, while worrying if you will ever be able to do them again, is not the best recipe for getting better—or for rewiring your brain! (#hellohardanddepressing)

I felt isolated, alone, and scared for my future. Everything I had dreamed of and planned for my future was taken away in an instant, with no promise of returning. I was in mourning for what I'd lost and unsure of who I was once the image I had of myself and my life so dramatically changed.

As a former "do, do, doer" and an overachiever, I found it incredibly hard to *rest* and *to give myself permission to do so.* If you are anything like me, you likely found this part the hardest too. In the beginning, I remember being at home and sleeping A LOT. It felt like the medications I had been prescribed to help with the pain actually made things worse. I would immediately fall asleep, or they would aggravate my already aggravating symptoms. I didn't *feel like me.*

And because I was sleeping all day, I would lie awake at night, frustrated. I remember sitting up with my dad as he worried, unsure of how to help, and me crying and crying, saying, "I can't cry anymore because crying makes my brain hurt and crying is bad for the brain." Yet crying was all I could do—there was honestly not much else.

And maybe that was the point, but we'll get to that. Because that, my friend, was the point of all the mud.

But right now, you are *in* the mud. In the thick of it. And when you're there, you don't want to hear someone telling you about the cake you can't eat or the dream you are afraid will never happen for you. You need the next step in the recipe first, not the whole damn cake.

Because healing takes time. It takes one step (or crawl or nap) at a time!

So, we have to start where we are.

Start where you are. Use what you have. Do what you can.

-Arthur Ashe

Right now, you are surrounded by a lot of mud, so let's dive in and find acceptance in it.

Facing our mud and learning to cleanse it means learning how to get real. Simply put, when we face the mud, we have to get real, and this is often the part we wish we could bypass. It's hard to recognize how we are truly feeling. We often try to look for the sunshine and rainbows when we are still in the middle of the storm.

But we have to share how we're really feeling in order to find a way through.

Just like the children's story *We're Going on a Bear Hunt* by Michael Rosen says:

"We can't go over it.

We can't go under it.

Oh no!

We've got to go through it!"

So, together, let's go through it. Because together is always better. But unlike the line in the story where the children say, "We're not scared," we're not going to lie. Like I said, let's get real. We're pretty scared right now, and that's okay.

Fear lives deep within the mud. And finding out what scares us most is indeed a step toward healing. Persian poet Rumi said, "The wound is the place where the light enters you." And as someone I know says: "Rumi never lies."

Thus, let's not start lying to ourselves now. Let's be kind to ourselves and befriend our fears (one step at a time). And our big feelings too.

So, let's start with the fears. Let's start with the mud . . . and let's start exactly where we are.

Remember, exactly who and where you are at this moment is more than enough.

You don't have to run from your fears anymore or run toward what you want but don't feel ready for yet.

You can walk first. What you are ready to do, though, is finally get real and honor it all.

TAKEAWAY & P L A Y

This is the part where we take the lessons for ourselves, take action on them, and let the book guide us to what we, personally, may be needing. This is where the real magic happens.

Before you keep reading on, I recommend you get an "Eat PLAY Love" journal of your own and your favorite pen. With an open heart and mind ready to love, to learn, and most importantly, to PLAY, let's start!

IT'S JOURNAL TIME:

- At this moment, **what is your biggest fear**? Give yourself the space to feel it, to name it, and to acknowledge the story that you are telling yourself. (Example: "My biggest fear is . . . The story I am telling myself is . . .")
- What is your mud?

Chapter 3

THE MUDDY WATERS THAT STARTED IT ALL

It is no coincidence that in most kinds of therapy, you get asked about your childhood. I clearly remember when I was asked that very big and loaded question: "What was your childhood like?"

If you've ever been to therapy, you likely have been asked this question too (probably more than once). So, just like Maria says in *The Sound of Music*—let's start at the beginning.

Let's go back to childhood because, as it turns out, it's a really good place to start. Although it's not always the easiest. Sometimes our inner child is scared to go back there, so we need to be patient.

I remember my own reaction when the therapist asked me to journey down memory lane; I was annoyed and confused. I didn't understand why it would help or how it had anything to do with my brain injury. I was there to heal my recent TBI, so why would we need to talk about my childhood?

Well, it turns out that my brain injury had a whole lot to do with my early years. I just didn't see it then. Nor was my childhood something I wanted to go back to.

When the therapist asked me the question that, for some, should be so simple, I froze. My mind went completely blank, and I couldn't answer it. I felt like I wanted to go anywhere but back to the beginning, like some part of me was trying to protect myself from going there.

I think a part of me also wanted my therapist to like me, and if I went back, I wasn't sure that she would. I was feeling too scared. Truthfully, I wanted to run or hide—maybe a bit of both. I had zero desire to share the parts of my past that weren't "happy." Those weren't the parts I believed made me worthy or lovable, and they weren't the parts other people wanted to hear about. So, I made up something about how my childhood was pretty normal, how I was a fairly happy kid, then I basically just sat there and cried. The thing is, no matter how hard I tried, I could no longer run. And I couldn't hide away from all the pain and trauma that had been suppressed for years. My tears said all the things I could not.

Looking back, this was a typical response for me when I was a child. Maybe my reaction in that moment was a glimpse into what my childhood was like: focusing on the happy parts and freezing up and crying anytime something "not so happy" occurred. This automatic fight-or-flight response was a normal part of my childhood. Except I always seemed to choose flight. Flight was more my style. Just like how I wanted to run the moment the therapist asked that question, I can remember literally running away when I was a child. And I would do just about anything to avoid a fight. Conflict avoidance was my way of staying "safe."

You see, as a sensitive kid, I really hated conflict. I didn't know how to deal with it. I couldn't handle it when people fought. I just wanted it to stop and for everyone to be happy again. When I was younger, I had a friend who bit me and tried to fight a lot while we were playing. We rarely got along, but I never understood why. I thought, *Why is she being mean to me? Why doesn't she like me? Why doesn't she treat me better?* I remember one time in particular when I finally had had enough. I was at her house "playing," and as usual, she was not being very nice to me. I started crying and ran all the way home in the middle of the afternoon. Fortunately, I happened to live around the corner and my mom worked from home. Both our mothers were frustrated by my actions that day, but even more so, they were worried. I think my parents worried about me a lot, mostly because of how sensitive I really was.

But that was how I coped—by running away, hiding away, avoiding and leaving any situation, person, or place that made me feel unsafe. Whenever things got heavy or out of hand, I would run away or hide and try to find "happy" on my own. This was evident in the way I played as well. I played with Barbies, and my Barbie story was always the same. Barbie and Ken would fall in love, get married, have lots and lots of babies and live happily ever after. Notice the *happy* part. When I played, everyone was happy; I could control that. So, playing became my safe and happy place. That is how I lived my life all through childhood: doing everything I could to keep everybody else (as well as myself) happy, because as long as people were happy, I felt safe on the inside.

As you can see, if I could sum up my childhood in one word, it would be SENSITIVE.

If you asked my parents, they would likely say the same. Or a mix of sweet and sensitive. Despite often feeling unsafe, I was also that kid who appeared happy, like a goofy kind of happy, and I was often excited to be around people. I loved people!

I was the kid who went to a sleepover and then would ask to go out and see another friend as soon as I came home the next day. I was social, I was kind, and I was a lover of spending time with others rather than spending any time with myself.

I think a part of me didn't even know what alone time was. I don't think I ever knew who I was if it weren't for who I was in relation to others. I relied on others' definition of me. My self-perception was dependent on who I was to them. I don't think I was just me—Amanda Evans. The real Amanda. I was Amanda, the student, the friend, the daughter, the sister. The sensitive soul. Amanda, the seemingly always happy and joyful one. Amanda, the one who was always there for you, no matter what. And it was all in an attempt to be well liked, accepted, and validated. Maybe that's why the therapist's question was so hard to answer. *Who was I? What was MY childhood like?*

Most of my childhood was spent focusing on others, playing with others, being around others, and wanting to be liked by others. I don't think I realized it at the time, but a lot of my childhood was spent not liking myself and avoiding getting to know who I was. I wasn't making time or space for just me; instead, I was trying to "fit in."

But I think I always had this underlying feeling that I didn't quite fit in. I think as children, all we want is to belong. Thus, as much as it may have seemed like I belonged on the outside, on the inside, I felt different. I felt like nobody really saw me or "got" me.

I was an old, sweet, and sensitive soul. The kid in the class who related more with her teachers than with the children her own age. The one who liked to hang out with older people. The one who always knew just how everyone else was feeling. The one who focused so much of her energy and attention on being a good friend, a good daughter, a good student. Dare I say perfect? You see, through most of my childhood I focused on how I could be the best, but on the inside, I didn't really feel like I was good at anything. I had the constant "not enough" feeling running on repeat inside. So, I would either run or hide, or do everything I could to get better, be better, or do whatever I could to feel like I finally fit.

Basically, my childhood consisted of what Brené Brown calls the three Ps: perfectionism, people-pleasing, and performing.

I don't think it's a coincidence that these coping mechanisms all start with the letter P, as they were my "patterns." We all have our own patterns, our ways of controlling a situation, our ways of staying safe, our ways of coping, and these were mine.

PERFECTIONISM

Let's start with this one. I was that kid who was not naturally good at the things, but if I practiced enough, if I worked hard enough, then I got really good at them . . . eventually. If I put all of me into something, there was no way I couldn't find a way. This was perfectionism at play. This might also be how I played as a kid.

I can't help but think back to junior kindergarten. I remember my mom's friend visited us. She had a daughter around my sister's age. This daughter was in all sorts of dance classes and acrobat classes too. I also had a friend who was a gymnast, as was her mother. They were both flexible, and they could do things like perfect cartwheels and front and back handsprings. I wasn't able to do those things.

In grade one, we started a gymnastics club at recess. On one day, I came home determined to do the splits. I knew that "practice makes perfect," so I decided that day that I was going to do the splits for as long as I needed to until I got it just right.

That's what perfectionism was to me. This incessant need to get it "just right." And it took everything out of me. It also took the fun out of playing. Instead of just enjoying gymnastics club or a regular Saturday at home, I was determined to be able to "do" something. So, I did. I tried and I tried and I tried until I could finally do the splits.

After a whole day of forcing my body into the splits, I couldn't walk for the next few days. I had strained my body, overextended every muscle—mentally and physically—trying to be perfect at the splits. It hurt! The memory still stands strong as something FUN that became "un-fun" when I made it a "must do" rather than just enjoying it and recognizing that it was okay that my body needed more time to learn to stretch that way.

PEOPLE-PLEASING

People-pleasing involves bending and stretching yourself (in another way) to get people to like or approve of you. I did that a lot.

People-pleasing often goes hand in hand with being sensitive. I never really knew (as a kid) that I was doing it. I also didn't understand that the way I experienced life wasn't how everybody else experienced it.

I always felt like I knew what everybody was feeling or what they were thinking. It was my way of staying safe. There is this idea of what safety is. We think of safety as being a lot of things. Sometimes we chalk up safety to the usual: having a home, a roof over our head, food to keep us nourished and healthy, and family or friends who love us. I had all those things. Yet there was another level of safety I did not feel.

The truth is, safety is a feeling we cultivate within us. There is also safety when it comes to how we feel in our body, how we feel in our family, how we feel with our friends and in the world. Do we feel safe to be ourselves? To be real, to be messy, to be imperfect, to say the wrong or imperfect thing?

That is a safety piece too. Or do we feel like we need to do the right thing or the good thing to feel like we are approved of and that we can be loved and accepted just as we are?

That's how my childhood felt. I looked for that internal feeling of safety by seeking it outside of myself.

I honestly didn't know which feelings were mine and which feelings were those of other people. I thought I had to control the room—make everybody else feel better in order to feel safe myself. If my parents were fighting, I believed it was my responsibility to fix it or to make them see each other's point of view. The same thing was true in my friendships. I was the glue. I hated when people fought. I was that kid who just wanted everybody to get along.

Remember the movie *Mean Girls*? Yep, I was like that character in the scene toward the end who was crying and saying, "I just wish we could all get along like we used to in middle school. I wish I could bake a cake made out of rainbows and smiles, and we'd all eat it and be happy." That was me.

Except that was definitely not the reality of middle school. Not mine at least. Middle school cemented the belief that girls are mean, but not in the "I'm being mean to your face and saying what's real" kind of way. It was the "fake smiles when you're around and talk about you behind your back and run away from you" kind of mean. That was my experience. For me, middle school was a time of walking on eggshells, stuffing down and ignoring my feelings, and wanting to be friends with the girls who were pretty and popular on the outside, so I could be too. I also wanted to feel good about myself. Truthfully, I didn't. I also had this compassionate side that just saw the good in everyone—even if sometimes a friend's disrespectful actions toward me outweighed the good I continued to focus on.

So, somewhere along the line, the people-pleasing pattern started. I remember girls running away from me who were supposedly my friends. I remember people treating me kindly one day and not the next. I remember not really understanding that behavior and never feeling like I could stand up for myself. Allowing myself to feel angry and navigating the wobbly uncertainty felt unsafe to me.

Being alone felt unsafe. Being friends with people and having them like me felt emotionally safer, even if they weren't the right fit for me. Having this felt safer than being alone. Or having that uncomfortable feeling inside knowing that people didn't like me, knowing what they were thinking or feeling—like if they were mad at me or didn't approve of the choices I made. I just wanted those uncomfortable feelings to go away! So, I let things that were not okay, be okay—and for the record, that is so not okay!

Never allow anyone to make you feel less than, unsafe, or disrespected, or to cross your personal boundaries. That is never all right. It is all right to wobble through it, knowing you are worthy of honoring yourself! But if this feels scary, bear with me . . . we will work through it together!

You might be wondering what I was afraid of. Wanna hear the truth? I think deep down, all that being with others was because I was afraid of being alone and having to see how unkind I actually was to myself. I was afraid of confronting the fact that I didn't like myself at all, which is why I had this incessant need for others to like me as a result. It was my way of making up for poor self-esteem and a lack of self-love.

I didn't like the way I looked, the fact that I was always just a little less smart than the girl I compared myself to, that I was just a little (or a lot) chubby and not really good at sports, or that I didn't have a "thing" like my friends did (dance, karate, singing, or "something" that made them seem more worthy). Being smart was my thing, but there was always someone smarter. Thus, somewhere along the way, being the "good girl" and the "nice kid" became my way of coping with the not-so-nice world and really, the not-so-nice girls. I became friends with the mean girls and found the niceness in them. I didn't speak up or stand up for myself when the friends I had treated me with disrespect. I thought I was made to be nice to everyone! Maybe that was my thing! It was as if on some subconscious level, I knew that if I was nice to everyone and friends with them, then they couldn't be mean to me, make fun of me, or call me names. If I fit in, then I was worthy and lovable too.

PERFORMING

We've touched on this one a little already. My incessant desire to feel worthy and lovable based on outward standards always meant striving for more. Do more, be more, have more. More, more, more. It was a lifelong quest. If I didn't get a perfect score on my dictée or all the stickers like the top student, then I would have to work harder. And it often did not come as easily to me as it did to her, even though I stayed up late doing my homework (something that started as early as grade three, maybe even grade one).

And it continued. I remember my mom feeling upset and being worried about me because I pulled all-nighters writing essays, doing book reports, and finishing homework because it would take me so incredibly long to get it done or to get it all "just right." Because it was as if nothing was ever quite good enough.

As it turns out, at the end of this session with the therapist, I got to the heart of the matter—the story that had been running my life: a "not good enough" story. And I finally saw why suffering a brain injury was so hard for me. It made those three Ps nearly impossible to achieve. It made being the "me" that I had become accustomed to all those years impossible to be.

I realized, then, that going back to my childhood was exactly what I needed to do.

TAKEAWAY &

IT'S JOURNAL TIME:

- If you had to sum up your childhood in one word, what would it be?
- What Ps (patterns) were your coping mechanisms when you encountered conflict, and how did you navigate childhood?
- Did you see yourself in any of the patterns described in this chapter?
- And did any of my stories bring back memories of your childhood?

Let them come up, without judging them or doing anything with them. First, just be aware. Just notice.

- What were the themes?
- How did you show up when you were feeling big emotions?
- What was your response and how might this play a role in how you are responding now?

TAKEAWAY & PLAY

The first thing I want you to do is name them. You are not your pattern. It's just something that you started doing to protect some part of you. Some part that felt not enough or something you do because you want love, you want safety, you want to know that being you is enough. So, let's not shame this out of you. But I guarantee, the next chapters will help if these patterns pop up as you navigate your lotus journey. In the meantime, here are some things you can do:

- First, name it (i.e., People-pleasing: This is the pattern showing up for me!).
- Then get clear on why this pattern is showing up.
- What is it trying to do or protect you from? How is this pattern serving you in some way?

Then get curious and compassionate.

- How do you need to meet and greet yourself at this moment?
- How do you need to meet your own needs rather than expecting some external person or experience to meet these needs for you?

If it's safety, how can you find that safety within yourself?

TAKEAWAY & P L A Y

Ask yourself: "If I felt completely safe, what would I be doing/saying/embracing/sharing instead? How would I be showing up? What might I start doing? How might I show up new? How would I communicate?"

Then lean in.

Give yourself grace, as this is unlearning a big pattern that has served you for a long time.

Breathe, greet yourself with gentleness, and start doing things a little differently.

One step, one imperfect action, conversation, or situation at a time.

And stay tuned on how to embody a little bit more compassion. Because shifting these patterns really is compassion in action.

And you deserve compassion. You've endured a lot, and you don't need to perfect getting over these past patterns. It's enough to just simply do your best.

Chapter 4

DO, DO, DO . . . UNTIL YOU CAN'T DO ANYMORE

Rest. Pause. Or in other words, don't do, just be.

By now, you are probably realizing that your Ps have made it hard to ever just be, especially when it comes to being who you once were. You likely have been spending a lot of time doing, achieving, bending, and being the person everyone else wants and expects you to be. And if you're a little like me, you have rarely spent time just being with yourself.

So, there I was in the dark, being faced with ME for the first time. I was sitting in a dark room with myself: my thoughts, my fears, my worries, and a whole lot of pain. Truthfully, I wanted to be anywhere but there. I wanted to escape my thoughts and fears and just focus on something that gave my life meaning. I wanted some way I could focus on everyone else because up until that moment, I felt like everyone else mattered more than I did.

Truthfully, this reality made having a brain injury, and anything else

I needed support with, really hard to receive. I needed help, I needed love. I needed extra support, compassion, and care, and I was used to being the one who gave these to others. In the past, I never wanted to ask for help. I wanted to be the helper, so needing others to be there for me was not something I was used to—or comfortable with.

I was uncomfortable in every sense of the word. And sitting there in the dark just made me wonder whether I would ever get better. Who was I now? If I really didn't like me when I thought being smart made me worthy—how would I like me now that I lost that? And if I needed other people to like me in order to feel good about myself, how would that work now considering that I physically couldn't be around people or truly be a present friend, daughter, or coworker in their life? All the roles I once played were not roles I could physically, emotionally, or mentally play anymore.

The "me" who could show up and be there was nowhere to be seen, and my symptoms and challenges were invisible. Living a life where I was constantly striving to be my best made it really difficult for me to be in the same body that no longer worked as it once had. The brain that had allowed me to do all these things no longer worked that way. Everyone still saw me as being the same, but on the inside, I wasn't that girl anymore.

So, I wanted to do anything I could to get better as quickly as I could to get back to the me that I used to be. I would lie in a dark room, then try and return to "normal" life as slowly as I could, one little activity at a time.

I tried to pick one thing a day to do, then rest afterward until I felt like my symptoms had gone away or gotten better, then I'd add another thing. But I struggled with this one a lot. Even if the symptoms had gotten a bit better while resting, it was the constant need to always be doing something, anything, that brought my pain right back. And lying in the "nothingness" didn't really help either because I worried whether I would ever get back to the things that made me, ME again. And I wondered if anyone would ever truly understand and "see" me again.

I realized in this darkness something I wasn't willing to face until that moment: For a good girl who appeared happy on the outside, there was a lot of darkness, sadness, and pain left unattended to on the inside. Like I did as a kid, I wanted to run from it. Or to distract myself from it until it would go away.

I remember once wondering whether I was an emotional hoarder. It was as if the hard moments or feelings in life had just been buried deep inside so I wouldn't have to face them. And in the dark room, alone with my thoughts, feelings, and pain, I had to see it all. And I didn't like what I was seeing.

When I was supporting others, working in a job that I enjoyed and was good at, being with the people I loved, and having friend time and family time, I was happy, and my pain didn't seem to be there. But in that dark room, that me didn't exist. The pain was the only thing there, and it was coming out in ways I couldn't ignore. I tried so hard to ignore it, to fix it, and to get to the bottom of it.

That's what perfectionists do when faced with mud. We see it and we want to get through it, so we try everything we possibly can. Psychotherapist Steven Kessler calls this way of functioning the "rigid pattern." I faced my brain injury and recovery the only way I knew how: by doing anything and everything I could to make it better.

I started off with the doctor's medications and protocols. I didn't like them one bit because the medications made me sleepy, less like me, and cognitively confused. I had a hard time listening to someone who I felt didn't fully understand me and how I was feeling or who couldn't hear me because my truth was not something I could easily express at appointments. My doctor kept telling me to rest and to try different dosages of medication. But I was frustrated because the medication continued to make everything worse. And it was a lot harder for me to do the things I needed to do.

I tried new ways of managing my pain and cognitive issues, all the while trying to get back to my "normal life," a.k.a. a part-time job and my big dream of finishing university so I could be a teacher. I struggled a lot when I made the choice to go back to my part-time job. I thought it would be a good idea to finally get out of that dark room and be part of life again. But life was harder with these new challenges and my "new brain."

I was exhausted by everything, and anything that caused me stress escalated the physical pain. It was like there was a constant stress button being pressed in my body at all times. I couldn't turn it off. Whenever a trigger became activated, my brain would feel overwhelmed and my whole body would shut down—all from the stress induced by my injury. I was on high alert, and the littlest things were telling my brain to stress and not rest.

This was "fight or flight" on repeat. All day, all night, all the time. And my attempts to try and fix me did just the opposite. It continued to keep me stuck in this state.

When we focus only on fixing and being constantly on the go, our cortisol levels spike, which keeps us in a never-ending state of fight or flight. Our adrenals are damaged, and we live in our sympathetic nervous system, staying in a constant and stressful state of "survival."

When we are in this stress-induced state, our bodies can't heal.

I didn't understand this. I thought I was doing all the right things! But maybe "doing" was actually the problem. And maybe my brain really needed this message to sink in: *Amanda, you don't need to be on high alert all the time. You don't need to have your "freak out right now" alarm bells turned on. It is safe for you to switch off, unplug, take a nap, and return to a balanced state.*

My body and mind needed to come back to a state of homeostasis. Like I said, I was far from "home," and homeostasis was just not my thing. Often, when trauma occurs, our brains don't always get the right messages; they can over-exaggerate something little. This is a typical response, especially when you have lived a life of constantly being in overdrive, overdoing, and perfecting, but then get hit with something major that stops you in your tracks, like a brain injury.

Your predisposition to stress and your fight-or-flight response turns your trauma into the perfect storm, making you stay in this state and creating this loop inside the neural networks of your brain. That's why I wasn't getting better. Because of stress. And forcing myself to get better within a finite time (while doing and trying everything) just caused more stress.

But I was super determined to keep going. So, I did. I went back to school the September after my accident and found out the hard way that despite my positive thinking that my brain would be okay, the reality was far from it. I remember going to class and realizing that nothing made sense. I could hear what the professor was saying, but the meaning would get lost somewhere after the information came into my brain. I had trouble translating and conveying my understanding of that information on paper.

And after class, I would feel so tired that I couldn't even get home, so I would nap on a couch somewhere on campus before regaining the energy to keep going and take the bus home so I could sleep again. I could barely hold a conversation or hang out with my roommates because doing so brought on more pain. Thus, I would take more meds and sleep again.

I eventually realized that school was not a good place for me, and I needed to learn more about how my brain worked in its post-accident state before I could actually get back to work. So, I dropped most of my courses that semester and only finished with two half credits, which I did horribly in, I might add. I moved home the following semester to live with my parents.

Together, we found a neuropsychologist and other alternative approaches to support me through the challenges I was experiencing. I was angry and frustrated, and I felt left out and behind, yet I still did my best to seem like I could do everything and keep it all together.

But I was barely holding anything together, and I deeply feared that I might never be able to live the way I always wanted to. It was as if everyone was living, and I wasn't part of it. I feared that I wouldn't be a part of normal social settings or live like everyone else or join them in anything. There it was again, that desire to truly belong, to be accepted, and to be well liked. I feared not being a part of something, anything.

All I wanted to do was go back to the life I had before the accident—to being the person I used to be. You could say that I was resisting with all my might the new me, the true me that was dying to emerge from within. That semester off from school, I learned about my brain and how to manage and cope with the way it now worked. It was slower. It needed more breaks and rest. It needed more support. I learned new ways to manage my pain and exhaustion. I had neuropsychological assessments with the psychologist and saw her for some support with the emotional side of things, because I was beyond sad, I was depressed. I felt like a big burden.

Those tests and those sessions just made me feel worse. I felt stupid, and the pain was indescribable. I felt bad for how much my family had to support me, and all I wished was that I could be better. I felt guilty and ashamed for receiving care and help.

My mom and dad sought out a lot of alternative ways of helping me since I shared that the medication was not something my body (or mind) was happy with. I remember my mom trying alternative ways to help with the pain, so we went to a naturopath. I tried a bunch of supplements and a clean diet to help my body heal. Maybe taking out gluten, dairy, and sugar would help. I was willing to try anything.

I went to an osteopath and an acupuncturist, who stuck needles in every part of me, head to toe. My sadness bubbled up, and I cried during and after, but I didn't feel much better physically. (I didn't realize at the time that such emotional releases were part of the healing process, but I was still resisting any strong emotions and not letting them come up fully, continuing to stuff them deep inside.)

I was constantly stressed and unable to truly rest and be there with my feelings—without focusing on where I wanted to be: back at school, with my friends, being the me that I used to be.

After taking a whole semester off and learning about how to navigate being the me I had now become—with my challenges and my "new" brain—I tried to get back to school. I knew learning would look and feel different this time around, so I had to use the tools and strategies I had received to work in a new way. I took only one course at university, and I was doing better than I had earlier that year. One course was manageable. One course I could do! It still meant every day was spent learning, studying, and resting, something I did on repeat. I "played" and socialized very little. My routine was to wake up, read, learn, rest, repeat! Eventually, I learned I could take on a bit more, so I added a few more courses. I wanted to see how it would go.

I kept going, I kept moving forward, I kept doing. Did I get better? Nope. Not at all. I just got better at accepting this way of living (or not living). I got better at surviving, but it wasn't living. **I wasn't living. I was doing, then resting.** Every day. I didn't realize it at the time, but I was in a constant state of fight or flight.

This time, however, my fight-or-flight response was me fearfully avoiding anything that might cause me pain or overstimulation. I was avoiding feeling misunderstood and feared not being seen for me. Life felt like a constant fight—fighting against the challenges in my life, hoping that it would all get better once I achieved that next thing, goal (my dream job), or what I thought would finally make me happy.

Fast-forward two more years at school. I continued in this way: more school, more appointments, more protocols, and more pain management. I was still not living. At this point, I had visited several chronic pain specialists and underwent more neuropsychological testing. After the two-year mark post diagnosis, I was told that it was likely that I had "plateaued," which meant that cognitively, I wouldn't get much better. And physically, I was still a mess. I was depressed, but I was unwilling to rest and not keep going. The very concept of allowing myself to rest, to simply be, was more than I would ever be willing to sit with, to accept, to give into. It felt like there was never enough time! (Especially being so slow!) It was too hard to see that maybe the things I had always wanted to experience in life might never happen.

Additionally, more than anything, I wanted to be a mom one day. Since the summer of my accident, I also had stopped getting my period and had been experiencing a lot of hormonal disruption, polycystic ovarian syndrome (PCOS), and other associated symptoms. This fear of maybe never having that dream was more unbearable than anything. But rather than sitting with these potentials, I got into "go, go, go" mode—my attempt of wanting to control the outcomes in my life.

I remember my mom sharing the Serenity Prayer with me: "God grant me the serenity to accept the things I cannot change, the courage to change the things I can, and the wisdom to know the difference." I tried to remind myself of that daily.

There was a lot I felt like I could no longer control: my body, my brain, my health. So, I tried to focus on what I could. I tried to smile through all the pain and fear and focus on what I could. I could keep going toward what I felt was my biggest dream. I could keep working hard every day. I could keep trying all the protocols, specialists, and people who thought they could help me. I could try to move on with the "new" me. I could work and make moves every day toward the dream of being a teacher. So, I did that.

My last year of teacher's college was the "I'm almost there" year, and at the same time, it was one of the hardest years since my brain injury. I didn't feel like my lighter course load was really possible in my new setting. It was a new school, with new subjects, with new everything. And I had trouble with "new."

Having a routine and knowing what to expect every day helped me to function with my symptoms. I got really stressed out by "new," and transitions were difficult. I had more people to engage with and more opportunities to advocate for the things I needed to be able to function in those settings. That year was full of transitions, adjusting to change. New living arrangements, new practicum placements, new things to stress about, and new people to work with.

I needed to help them understand how I functioned and that how I looked was not at all how I felt or how I worked. That being in the classroom was a lot harder than I thought it would be. That this fast-paced environment was not the best place for my slow-paced brain. That every day I would come home stressed out and in pain.

And then I would do it all over again.

TAKEAWAY & PLAY

If this chapter was a difficult one for you, it's likely because you're realizing that you've been working really hard—doing and trying to get better—but it might not feel like any of it is working. I know how hard it is to let go of your worries.

This is a space for you. This is a place for you to finally pause. But I don't want to leave you pausing in your pain, in your biggest fears, or in your worries that you'll need to do it all again tomorrow.

So, I am going to help you pause in a new way. A new way to play: a short meditation. To drop into your "real" being, your body, and the beauty that can come from not doing and learning how to **BE**.

I've recorded a special meditation for you on my website. Go to the Resources at <u>https://www.mindbodysoulmiracles.com/eat-play-love</u> and listen to the meditation for Chapter 4.

- Press PLAY and simply listen.
- Let your whole body hear the messages of this meditation and relax into the knowing that you can be held, with all your fears/feelings right here, right now.

TAKEAWAY & P L A Y

- And no, meditation is not something you need to get right or get better at. This is your sacred pause and rest. There is no right or wrong way to do it!

Chapter 5

ROCK BOTTOM IN A BASEMENT APARTMENT

I felt like I was trying to crawl out from rock bottom. And based on everything I had been through, I was not going to stop until I got "there."

"There" being my dream to become a teacher.

Well, I got there.

Unfortunately, my idea that it would all get better once I achieved this dream was far from reality.

It was actually worse than how the last few years of being a student had been. Every day felt like "new" all over again. I was stressed. I struggled to keep up—with the curriculum, the planning, the changes, everyone's needs, and even with the pace of the school environment. "Slow" was not something that worked in this system. Neither were cognitive challenges. I could barely remember everyone's names, let alone remember their progress or what happened that day. Just being present took everything out of me, mentally and especially physically. I felt like an emotional mess.

I was doing my best. But my best did not feel good enough. I felt like a failure, every day. I would go home and cry. Sometimes I would cry in the bathroom at school. This wasn't at all how I thought it would be or how I would feel once I had my dream. I felt like I needed help all the time and like there was nobody to help me because everybody else was equally as stressed out, and I was the one who was supposed to have it all together.

New wasn't something I could do anymore—and in all honesty, I couldn't DO anything anymore! I was tired. I was ready to wave the white flag and surrender. Fight or flight could no longer be the way forward. My "do, do, doing" would no longer allow me to keep going, and my body was no longer willing to keep bending and breaking in the ways I had been forcing it.

I felt like there was no way through—all the ways I tried to cope, manage, and deal with life since my brain injury had occurred would not work here. *I could not work here.* It was like trying to master and nail the splits all over again. I had spent all that time learning how, finding a way, and I finally did it—but now I was paying for it.

The years leading up to the dream cost me the dream itself. I finally had my own classroom teaching kindergarten, and I felt like I had nothing left to give. *How could I support these little kiddos who needed extra love, attention, and care if I couldn't even give those things to myself?* And the question I kept asking myself was: **"What is the fucking point?!"**

I had spent the past few years pushing myself to be able to do this thing that I thought would make me happy, and I was the unhappiest I had ever been. And even worse, I gave up everything to be there. I wished I was anywhere but there. There in the town where I had moved for that job! A job I gave up because I could not be in that classroom anymore. A job that I thought would make me happy that instead gave me levels of anxiety I had never experienced before. A job I came home from every day to cry uncontrollably and worry about going to the next day.

So, there I was, asking myself questions, wondering why I gave up those years of hanging out with my friends, playing, and spending time with the people I love only to find out that the answer to the earlier fears of "is it worth it" was a big resounding NO!

It was dark. Like the dark basement apartment I was living in. I was stuck in a deep, dark, and damp place—you know, where the mud is the stickiest and it feels like you're trapped there forever and there is no way through.

Yet again, I did the only thing I knew how to do: take flight and avoid the emotions I was truly feeling. The depression I was in was very present. All I could feel every moment of the day was this BIG "feeling like a failure" emotion. My feelings were not something I wanted to experience. I was hiding, afraid to see anyone from the school where I chose to take a leave of absence, embarrassed that I could no longer do the job I had always dreamed of having. And that thing was the thing I was good at! And I couldn't even do that!

So, I continued to try to hide from the shame I felt, the deep, deep shame of feeling like I was bad at everything and like I had nothing of value to give or show for myself in this world.

I felt like a burden. Like my life served no purpose. I felt that since my life now served no purpose, I was somehow not worthy of being here, of being loved, of being supported.

It was during this rock bottom moment that I had this realization dawn on me: Up until then, I thought it was my purpose to exist for others. That my worth came from teaching, from supporting, from serving and giving other people's lives meaning. And without that, without doing anything for others, life had no meaning. I felt like I had no meaning. I actually wished I were no longer alive. I felt far from "alive." I wished I could just disappear and not be there. I wanted to be anywhere but there.

But there I was, in this moldy basement apartment, with my feelings, ALL my BIG FEELINGS.

So, I did what any depressed and out-of-hope person does: I binged Netflix so I didn't have to feel or think about what my life had become or where I would go from there. I wanted to find a distraction or try to feel something other than how I was really feeling.

I would cook, but even food didn't bring me the comfort or joy it once did. I used to eat my feelings, but this feeling felt awful. I felt sick to my stomach, so I didn't even want to eat. I didn't want to be.

It felt as if I were at my rock bottom, and I didn't know if I'd ever recover. All the running on repeat left me with this endless, hopeless, helpless feeling. But maybe that's exactly when you should press play. At least, that's when I did.

I remember lying there on my old brown couch, under a bunch of blankets with all the lights off (both on the outside and within me), and I felt like it was the perfect time to press play on the emotional movie *Eat Pray Love*. It was time to watch someone else have their own journey.

Something happened while I was watching it. I'm not even sure I can explain it. I remember watching Julia Roberts's character (Elizabeth

Gilbert) in her own rock bottom. It was her "bathroom floor" moment. The moment she knew she could no longer stay in her marriage; the moment she realized she needed a new way; the moment she prayed and asked God/Universe/Source for help, for anything to help her see her way out of her rock bottom moment.

I remember thinking that I hadn't prayed since I was a little girl. Whenever my grandma visited, she'd kneel by our beds before my sister and I fell asleep, and we would all pray together. But it wasn't something I ever did on my own. I don't know if I ever believed in prayer. But she did, and I liked the way we did that together.

This moment was much like that. But instead of my grandma, it was just me and Julia (Elizabeth).

As I watched her break down and kneel in her bathroom, tears streaming down her face, unsure where to go from where she was, something moved me. I had to join her, to kneel on my own basement floor and pray. Because I needed a new way. I was out of "ways," and I didn't know what else to do. So, I thought I may as well pray. This was the one thing I hadn't tried, so what did I have to lose?

I don't remember what I said or what happened next. In moments like these, it doesn't feel like anything big happens, but that is often when the biggest shifts take place. Because praying is actually asking for help. It's a form of total surrender into something beyond yourself. It's a way of allowing yourself to receive. And I think this was the first time I had started asking for help. I was no longer able to do things the way I had done them before. I was out of solutions I could come up with on my own. I was ready for more, or at least ready for anything beyond the reality I was experiencing.

I had given up.

That's the thing about rock bottom, though. There is only one way to go from there.

Up, and only up! Just like the Shania Twain song!

She was right. And Elizabeth Gilbert was onto something.

TAKEAWAY & P L A Y
(OR PRAY?!)

At this point, we need a new way.

And maybe like me, you are out of "ways" and ready for a new one!

- If you could ask for anything right now, what would it be? Have you reached your rock bottom and are you ready to go up?
- Are you open to prayer? Or asking for help in a way that makes sense for you?
- What do you need? What do you want? What would help you find hope again?

Ask for it now.

Don't worry about what to say or how to say it, but show up for you. Let it be okay that you are feeling like a mess right now, and that you don't have any idea about how you will get through it or feel like living again. But if you are here right now, you are ready for it. For the miracle. For the breakthrough. And sometimes all you have to do is ask.

TAKEAWAY & PLAY

Now is the time to ask. Repeat after me:

"I am ready. I am ready for a new way. I am ready to be guided. I am ready to be led."

Chapter 6

MAKING FRIENDS WITH YOUR BIG FEELINGS

I remember being at yet another appointment. I was in my "what is the point?" part of the journey. I couldn't shake my fear that I might not get better because I'd plateaued (thanks to my doctor's recent prognosis, two years after my accident). That story was how one person's belief became my own. I stopped feeling like there was a point to finding new ways, to finding people who could help me or would be able to support me to live the life I wanted. I felt like the life I wanted wasn't possible.

I wasn't into finding a solution, a new program, protocol, or practitioner. I was over it. I was also over having to go in and tell one more person "my story."

But then someone came along who wanted to dive into what was underneath the "story," the label or idea that I *was* my brain injury. She wanted to get to know me.

I think I did too. **It was time to get to know the real me.**

The me underneath all this mud, not the label that I felt I had become. I wasn't a brain injury, and **I wasn't a patient to be fixed, but rather a person to be loved, accepted, seen, and understood for who I was. And I was in need of a lot of love. And compassion.**

Up until then, it had been recommended that I see a few psychologists. I didn't like talking about my big feelings with people. I didn't feel like it ever helped me get anywhere or feel better about anything. I felt like it was just a place to talk about how much life sucked and how I wished things were different. I felt like I was just being whiny and not a "Positive Patty" like I had always been and so badly wanted to be.

But this time was different. I was ready to get underneath (or really deep into) the mud and find out what was real. Truthfully, the only reason I went to see this new therapist was because someone I deeply looked up to, loved, and wholeheartedly respected had seen her before. My friend told me that in a difficult time in her life, she went to see this therapist.

Seeing her helped my friend find a new perspective and have a safe space to move through what felt difficult to navigate. My friend told me that it helped having someone who listened and who held space for it all.

I don't know if I had ever had this safety and acceptance being all of me with someone before except with this friend. She was that person for me in my life up until that point. So, if this therapist could help her, then maybe I could try seeing her. If this therapist could hold the person who held me, then maybe I could let her hold me too.

I was resistant, but I think the breadcrumbs led to me saying yes. Sometimes we are resistant to the things that are actually going to help us, the things that will catapult us into our growth and healing. When we have tried so many things and nothing has seemed to work, we are afraid to try anything else. We feel like there may not be a point or that we are wasting our time and/or money. So, we'd rather stew in our feelings—of feeling ashamed and as if we are a failure—all by ourselves so nobody else has to be let into it.

It turns out that that's the perfect time to let someone in. And it's also the perfect time to go within. Therefore, despite my own resistance, I booked that first appointment to get to know the therapist and to see if we were a "good fit."

I showed up, nervous, annoyed, and afraid about having to talk about all my feelings. I was afraid to let someone new in. But then I got there and realized it was different. This therapist was different from the psychologists I had met before. What I didn't know then was that she was a spiritual psychotherapist and that working with her was really my intuition guiding me on a spiritual journey.

At that point in my life my intuition wasn't something I was familiar with, but I was ready to meet her and finally let her in. I had prayed for a way, and in time, I was led to her. I think that might be how prayer works. You pray, and someone shows up. You ask for something, and you receive it. You surrender, and you are supported.

In this initial thirty-minute session, I had more clarity, understanding, and compassion than I had ever experienced, perhaps in my entire life. She cared. She "got" me. She understood not just where I was today, but also where I had been. And she made it easy for me to talk about that.

Except she did ask about my childhood.

We started that day by going *there*.

And I get it now. The reason why this time in my life felt so "life changing" was because I had never felt safe feeling, expressing, or processing my feelings. And because I never felt good enough or like I could still be worthy and lovable simply by being me.

I felt like I had to show the good parts, not the parts of me that felt too shameful, scary, or horrible to reveal. Up until then, I'd never fully felt safe to be seen or to be all of me. I felt like I had to get it "perfect" (remember all those Ps?).

I learned about the ego and realized that mine had been playing the lead role in my life; hence why losing all the roles, identities, and "specialness" that the ego loves made it feel like I was dying inside. In a way, maybe I was—and like I said, maybe that was the point.

I needed to let someone see all these parts so I could put the puzzle that was me back together again or maybe together in a way that it had never been before. Maybe I was building a new puzzle. I think we forget that sometimes the only thing we need is the next piece of the puzzle. And she was that for me.

She was my guide. I had been led in that moment of complete surrender to someone who could help me make sense of my mess and find a little meaning in it.

We started by diving off the deep end: into my deep, heavy feelings. I was no longer hiding from them and was instead talking about them. Feeling them, crying through them (there was a lot of crying!). Every time I got there, I would cry, use an entire box of tissue, then leave dehydrated from the tears that I'd shed. What I didn't realize was all the pent-up emotions I had been hanging onto for dear life, my whole life, were finally being released. I no longer needed to hang onto what was never mine to carry. I no longer needed to hoard my feelings.

I felt safe with her. I felt safe to be all of me: the sad, the ashamed, the guilty—the parts of me that were unexpressed up until this point in my life were easily expressed with her. She helped me to make friends with my feelings.

I say "friends" because when we become emotional hoarders like I had been, feelings are not our friends. We don't get to know them, ask them questions, or listen to them. We ignore them and make excuses for them, just like those people who I used to think were my friends. They didn't treat me with love and respect, nor did I treat my own feelings that way. It was time to start becoming really good friends with my feelings and being there for what they needed—and let them be there for what I needed. Thus, I sat in the therapist's office every week and shared. I shared all of it, all of me, and together, we became friends with my feelings.

She was more of a coach than a therapist. She was on my team. She was my cheerleader on the sidelines of my life and on my journey. She guided me along, gave me books to read and journaling to do. She supported me in the way she intuitively felt like I needed at that moment. She knew. She knew this was a *journey*, an awakening, an unlearning. She was good at letting me learn what I needed to in my own timing, though. A good coach and teacher always knows. They are there for you and are there to support you, without doing the work for you. They hold space for your personal growth and transformation and guide you to go within, to hear yourself louder than any other voice.

As I have shared, "within" was never a safe space for me, and I had never learned how to go there. I was scared of going there and learning to just be with me. But I didn't have any other way. So inward I went. And reading was a new way I moved through it. And after my injury, reading hurt my head, and I felt as if I was really slow. But I listened. I picked up the first book the therapist recommended and started to journal. I began to feel and express all that was, up until then, unexpressed.

I remember the day she recommended a book called *Self-Compassion* by Kristin Neff.

I was confused. I thought I knew about compassion. I thought I was good at compassion. I was caring toward everyone else: my friends, my family, the little ones in my life. **But I had never put the words *self* and *compassion* together.** The only association I made with anything that even remotely resembled self-love, a.k.a. putting myself and my needs first, setting boundaries with others, and advocating for what I need was "selfish." *How dare I start caring for myself and loving myself?* This question often surfaced when I thought of doing something for me. I had never given that same deep love, acceptance, and compassion to myself. I didn't know it was allowed or even encouraged. I was horrible to myself. I blamed myself. I spoke unkindly to myself; I kicked myself while I was down, and I felt like I was a waste of a person in the world.

I also carried a lot of guilt: guilt for being alive and having people care for me and spend their money on me to get better. Guilt for leaving a classroom of sweet children without a teacher and creating chaos in an already chaotic setting. Guilt for not being able to work and for no longer being able to do the thing that I had always thought was what gave me worth in this world.

So, I read Neff's book, little bits at a time. One page at a time, sometimes just one chapter at a time (depending on my day), and one exercise at a time. Then I got to this exercise:

I was instructed to write a letter. But not a letter to another person like I would have thought.

A letter to me. Kind of like a love letter to me.

She had instructed me to write a letter to myself, as if I were writing it to a friend.

We are often kinder, more understanding, more compassionate, and more loving toward others than we are to ourselves. I had been that way with others and was not giving myself that same grace to fall, to fail, to pick myself back up again, or to simply be where I was and let that be okay. Let not being okay right now be totally okay.

What would I say to a friend going through this hardship? This moment of unbecoming, this moment of working their way up from the bottom, this moment of not being the person they once were but becoming someone new?

How would I speak to them?

What did they need to hear?

This was the point of that letter. To write to myself about all that I had been through, all that I was enduring, and choose words with loving kindness to support and understand myself through this challenging time. To share all the things that I so badly wanted another to share with me, but to let it come from me. To use kind words, patience, gentleness, and gratitude for myself, for where I had been and how I was getting by, doing the very best I could, and to let myself know that that was enough. And that I am enough. To give myself permission to not be perfect, permission to simply be. Be where I currently was. To no longer take on the guilt and shame I was carrying, but instead give myself love and acceptance through it all.

So, I sat down, I wrote, then I read it aloud.

I began to understand just how hard on myself I had always been. How badly I needed these words that came from deep within. How much I needed to feel compassion for myself, for my mistakes, for my mud, and for how I had done my best at moving through it.

I read it aloud and cried.

But these were different tears; these were "I finally see you, I'm here for you, and I love you" tears. These were the "I know you were trying your best and you don't have to carry it all anymore" tears. These were tears of deep reverence, love, and acceptance for all the places I'd been and for exactly who I am today.

TAKEAWAY & P L A Y
(AND LOVE YOURSELF RIGHT WHERE YOU ARE!):

It's time to write yourself a love letter.

Write those words that you so badly need to hear right now.

- Maybe it's "I forgive you for _____" or "I love you" or "I see you and how hard you tried."
- Maybe it's a permission slip for not having it all together, not needing to be perfect.
- Or perhaps it's a forgiveness letter for feeling like your worthiness and love came from another or from *doing* rather than from deep within (and for simply *being*).

Whatever you need to hear about your own personal mud right now is what this letter is all about.

What would your best friend say to you? How would they comfort you, nurture you, love you, accept you? Add a little more compassion to your words.

This time, it's for you, from you.

You don't need to share it with anyone, but you can. Sometimes it can be extra healing to let someone into your "shame" because shame loses its power when shared.

TAKEAWAY & PLAY

Write your self-compassion letter and read it aloud. Just be with yourself and let your feelings guide you forward. Let the words on the page touch your heart. Let the "broken" parts of you be loved and accepted, exactly as they are. You don't need to change anything—just be with it, with all of you. That's the next best step.

Chapter 7

WHEN WE PAUSE, WE HAVE THE CHANCE TO PIVOT

So here I was, reading books and starting to learn about self-compassion. I learned about a lot of things through the books my therapist gave me. One of the most memorable books was *Untethered Soul* by Michael A. Singer. I also remember reading and learning more about the ego.

Reading and deeply reflecting on all that Eckart Tolle had to tell me in his book *The Power of Now* left me with clarity. If you've been guided to him or any of his work, you know he is all about embracing the present. It turns out, most of my life, I had been giving my power to the past and the future—my fears and worries—and never the present moment. Never the here and now. Never savoring it. Never *being* fully in it. Always focused on what others thought of me or what they would think of me. All my thoughts my entire life revolved around pleasing other people, performing for everyone else, and with that, fixating on everything, including myself, being perfect.

Of course, it was hard to let go of control and stay present and enjoy each moment for what it was. But just how does one simply stay in the present moment? It perplexed me at first.

I was always busy. Busy doing, busy thinking, busy being in my head and in the "there is not enough time" state of mind. Slowing down and pausing was not something I had learned or that felt good. I remember many naturopaths and people over the years recommending meditating, but like most people who could really use meditation, I'd say, "I don't have time to meditate!"

I was too busy to meditate. I was always looking at the next thing on the to-do list that needed my immediate attention. Time was not something I had enough of, and I was always wanting more.

But now, I had time. I wasn't working. I wasn't doing as much, and I would do anything to get better, including meditating (which in a way is not doing, rather *being*).

During one of my sessions with my psychotherapist, she guided me through meditation for the first time. It was fascinating. It was like light would enter into me and my pain would go away slightly, but then it would get stuck in my head—and not move out. Kind of like me: being stuck in my head, my fears, and my worry! I didn't see the connection at first. All I knew was that for some reason, my headache would get worse.

But I did feel really calm. Really peaceful. I would think, *So this is what it's like to JUST BE!* I liked it. **This was a new feeling**. But I didn't like how much my head hurt at the beginning. I was willing to keep trying, though, to see what would happen.

Like I said, I'd try anything!

I remember being told to start small. Start with a timer for five minutes of meditation, then after a while, do ten minutes. I got an app for meditating and would do it first thing in the morning and again before bed. That was the beginning of a beautiful meditation relationship.

Despite the fact that I had started meditating, I still wasn't fully pausing. I still had a lot of ego running the show that felt like I needed to get back to work, get back to doing, get back to being of "value" in some way. So, I accepted that maybe I wasn't able to go back to the classroom as a teacher, but I was willing to explore maybe going to a different type of classroom.

Maybe if I wasn't teaching as many children or doing so much academic (thinking) work, it would be a bit better. I was grasping to try and hold onto *something* that would give me my worth, some external praise or feeling of good enough.

I had a mentor who was happy to hire me to teach at a preschool instead. I remember feeling really hopeful about FINALLY feeling good about myself again—having a purpose, having a focus. The thing is, I had been showing up for this journey, for this unlearning and dying of the ego, so I could be the me that I truly was underneath what I thought was me. That said, it was still tempting. I was really considering it, thinking maybe it was the perfect solution. I'd work and do something else and "everything would be fine!" I was stressed about making this decision. It was around that time that the Universe sent me a message. An unwanted and very LOUD message (thank you very much!).

I was at home and the weirdest thing happened. I was walking and the next thing I knew, I was on the floor. I must have hit my toe on the door or the wall or something. I literally can't tell you what happened exactly. All I know is that I was up, then I was down. It was like I fainted or lost consciousness, then I broke my toe. Like "really gross, bone completely bent and insanely painful" kind of broken toe. This would surely slow me down . . . you would think.

So, I broke my toe, big deal. Maybe I could still do that other job.

You see, one of the things I learned in therapy is that "what we resist, persists."

I was still resisting the PAUSE.

I kept trying to pivot without honoring the pause. And the pause is sometimes the whole point. The pause gives us the chance to slow down, to go within and get to know who we really are, and to learn to be and love the person who could just BE.

I showed up at therapy after the broken toe incident and told my therapist what happened. She just sat there, laughing. So hard. She said, "I think it's pretty clear, the Universe is telling you to slow the fuck down!"

That made me laugh!

I cried and laughed a lot in therapy. It was good for the soul . . . and my heart. And yep, maybe the Universe was telling me to slow down (whatever that really means). Maybe I didn't want to see it. Maybe I'd always seen those roadblocks as something that meant I just needed to try harder. Work harder. Or push harder.

But this time, I was listening. I had resisted pausing up until that moment, but then, with my broken toe, I literally couldn't move quickly or really do anything that involved walking, so maybe pausing was the only thing to do. I had no choice but to listen and pause.

So, for someone new at "pausing," this meant more meditating and reading books!

Time for a Plan B. I actually read Sheryl Sandberg's book *Option B*. How she felt really resonated with me. I may not have lost my husband, but somewhere along this journey, I had completely lost me.

Maybe the brain injury was starting to teach me that "losing myself" wasn't such a bad thing. Maybe the me that I had been, the one who lived with those three Ps and many patterns, wasn't really who I was. Maybe it was just the "stuff" that I was carrying and that my ego so badly wanted to cling to.

Maybe Eckhart Tolle was onto something, claiming that the present moment, that simply being, is the point of life.

Maybe the reason for the brain injury, the broken toe, or everything, really, is that there is meaning in every little thing.

There is an excerpt in *Untethered Soul* that sent shivers down my spine: "You'll see that situations will unfold and hit your stuff. But in truth, that's exactly what has been happening your entire life. The only difference is that now you see it as a good thing because it's an opportunity to let go."

Whoa! How can you not *Whoa!* after reading that truth bomb!

I remember the first time I read it, and it hit me . . . right in the ego!

It was time to let go.

That excerpt meant that situations will unfold that may activate us, trigger us, hit our "stuff," and force us to confront and sit with our shit. Of course, my therapist liked to swear and changed "stuff" to "shit." I, having been the "perfect people-pleaser uptight sweet teacher kind of good girl" rarely swore. But something about this unlearning called for swearing. It felt like when I'd drop an f bomb, I was speaking truth. So, we called it "shit" because there was a lot of "shit" being hit. But maybe the shit was always a call for a *shift*.

And pausing was the step that was necessary to simply learn to be with it all. The stuff. The shit. The false me. So, I could start to learn to uncover and love the me that's left. The shit is all the mud that's simply creating space for the lotus to emerge.

In his book, Singer also writes, "You will not be able to solve anything outside until you own how the situation affects you inside."

I guess it was time to go inside. Maybe the problem itself wasn't so much the brain injury, but how I responded to it. And what I made it mean about myself. How I coped with, tried to fix, perfect, perform, and resist what this shift was trying to teach me.

TAKEAWAY & P L A Y

As you may have guessed, this entire book is about your shift. Taking your shit and making it the greatest fucking shift you have ever experienced. It's time to go inward. **Turn your "shit happens" moments into a "shift happens" breakthrough!**

Pause. Be. Have compassion for yourself. It might feel like a time-out right now, but it's the Universe giving you a time-in. And you deserve a time-in. To let love in too.

Do your best to stop resisting the learning and shifting that is working its way through you. To see the situations, the accident, the trauma as the door opening for you—to learn to see you, to be with you, to love you, and to *finally* just fucking pause.

Let's pause and go within.

- It's time to learn to meditate. One little meditation break at a time.
- Tune in and let go, with an open heart.
- It's time to start: Head to the Resources at https://www.mindbodysoulmiracles.com/eat-play-love and begin a meditation practice (however aligns and is most supportive for you, whatever stage you are in!).

TAKEAWAY & P L A Y

- You can start with five minutes and build up from there. That's what I was guided to try during my journey. I slowly built up until I reached twenty minutes after waking up and twenty minutes before bed. (Or even more when I felt like I needed a little extra "being" time!)

- If you are also looking for apps or other meditation resources (and my meditation voice is not your jam), no worries! Head to the Resources section at the back of the book and check out some of my favorites (Calm and Insight Timer are both good for beginners; Headspace was the app that I used; and personally, I love a good meditation by Gabby Bernstein!).

Chapter 8

WHEN THE STUDENT IS READY, THE TEACHER WILL APPEAR

At the beginning of this book, I mentioned that we need to take the next step, add the next ingredient to the mix, and that's the only place we need to be. And let's be clear; up until this point in our journey, *doing* is all we have known. We are trying to find all the solutions or ways to "fix the problem." We may want to move forward, but it's like in every step we try to take, there is this fear that stops us from jumping in with both feet. We don't quite feel ready to jump yet—that's when your teachers appear. This chapter is about just that. It's about when you know you're on your way to something new, yet you still have some things to learn before you feel ready to put that last foot forward. Out of the past, out of the pain, and into the new.

Sometimes we try to skip ahead, jump in without a parachute, without support or help along the way (or pivot without pausing), but right now, simply be here. Let your next step in the recipe come to you. This may be new for you; welcome it!

When you are ready for something, the Universe always finds a way to bring you and whatever "it" is together. Even if you don't *feel* "ready." I know I wasn't, and that's when the Universe got to work (or had its fun playing with me! It was more like that than anything).

The Alchemist by Paulo Coelho talks about how when you *really* want something, "the whole Universe conspires in helping you to achieve it." *This* is the part when we stop achieving and we start allowing in what we need most. Allowing ourselves to experience the shift: to be guided, to be held, to "be," all the while being seen and supported . . . so you can eventually take your foot out of the old and fully step into the new.

> *What you seek is seeking you.*
> *–Rumi*

And my personal favorite motto:

> *When the student is ready, the teacher will appear.*
> *–Siddhartha Guatama Shakyamuni*

At least, that's how it was for me, and I have a pretty good feeling that's how it will be for you too (if it isn't already). So, let's walk through what I mean by that—and I say walk because we aren't going to run or jump before we learn to walk . . . one step, crawl, appointment, or cry at a time! I am assuming there have been A LOT of appointments, and if you're like me, a lot of tears too.

You might be feeling like you've tried just about everything. You might be feeling like there's no point in even trying one more thing, one more protocol, one more practitioner, one more book, or one more way. That's why you prayed or finally asked for a new way.

When you prayed, you surrendered.

That means you have no idea what is coming your way—but you deeply trust that whatever it is, is meant for you, and working for you, happening for you. You are finally starting to get out of your own way. Yet even in this new state of surrender, your mind might still get in the way, trying to control, living in the fear and worry of "what if none of this works" because you remember that in the past, it didn't (or at least it felt like it didn't).

But here's the thing: It may not have worked because you were working (or worrying) so darn hard—to heal, to have it all together, and to be the perfect patient. This is when you need a new way. Often, as we are being guided to a new way, we end up going through a wobbly hero/ heroine's journey of feeling stuck in the old while wobbling through the new. If this is you, be there for the wobbles, and let the Universe hold you in the vision of your new way. It will make sense, even if none of it does at this very moment.

This chapter is about the moments that don't exactly make sense but are exactly what they are meant to be and are perfectly aligned in the big picture. Let the people show up who are here to hold you through the awkwardness in between, and let yourself be wherever you are. Much like an awkward toddler learning how to crawl, walk, talk, and just be a learning human, be gentle with yourself. Your soul could use it.

You are unlearning old ways and learning new ways of viewing yourself and being with yourself, so give yourself grace.

Allow it to be however it is (even if some days it doesn't feel like learning). And in these moments, trust there is something your soul has to learn to prepare you to take flight into the new. **Let the teachers who show up in your life during these times be a guide for you.**

I think the Universe gives us signs, breadcrumbs, little moments of sending us in a direction that will support us, even when we don't believe. This is when we need them most! It's like someone somewhere is singing Journey's anthem "Don't Stop Believin'" on repeat, nudging us to simply try in our own journey.

This chapter is about the trying—when you are ready to try just about everything and yet still aren't quite where you really want to be. You continue asking the question, "Are we there yet?!" (It's really more like **why** aren't we there yet?) So, let the breadcrumbs do the talking until you start to do the walking, beyond the wobbling.

Examples of breadcrumbs might be that friend who mentions a specialist or person they have seen. Or perhaps you see a name or word appear multiple times until an aha moment clicks for you on the why. Or you feel the pull to read a certain book before you meet someone who is familiar with that philosophy and way of healing. Like this book, for instance. You picked it up or maybe you had breadcrumbs lead you to it. Or maybe someone you look up to, someone whose perspective you respect and appreciate, told you about it or you had heard my name a few times before you finally listened to the call to pick up the book.

That's what breadcrumbs are. The nudge that often comes a few times before you really hear whatever it is saying loud and clear. **Our brain thrives on repetition. Rewiring our neural pathways is a constant act of choosing repetition and compounding the habit of doing something new until it feels second nature.** So, if you notice something appear a few times, there is likely a reason why it continues to appear in your life. Let it guide you.

That was what happened to me. And sometimes when we are really aligned or guided to be somewhere, the signs and breadcrumbs will continue to find us until we FINALLY listen. And other times those nudges will feel like a push or a shove in seemingly weird ways, especially if we continue to be resistant to it. Welcome the weird! It has our backs!

There was a moment for me. A moment when I was led. When the student is ready, the teacher appears. When I finally surrendered and asked for help, I eventually had A LOT of teachers appear. In those moments, however, I didn't really know that they were teachers. I just assumed it was like the past: they were professionals, experts on me, my body, my sickness. I thought they held all the answers and the tools—that they were there to heal me. But it turns out they were there to guide me back to *me*. To help me find me, to help me learn to love me and let love in. And to learn to let others love, guide, hold, and be there for me too.

Since we still have one foot in the old, let me share and guide you through my wobbly journey and exactly what I was learning. At the time, I was resisting a lot too. So, stay open and put on your curious observer hat to notice where you may be resisting as well. Because if you are open, you will discover and learn that every person, encounter, and moment matters and will teach you or cause you to (potentially) hit your shit and to help you shift.

I already mentioned that when I was ready to finally make friends with and feel my feelings, I was guided to the psychotherapist who was ready to hold space for it all. She was my next step. Then when I was ready for a different way to heal, I was guided to practitioners and "my team." They were also there to hold me and help me find a new way.

But before any of those moments, any of those teachers, there were several people who tried to help me do the same. They were trying all the protocols and ways to heal the brain or really manage the many symptoms a brain injury entails. But underneath all the trying, all the doing of things, I was dying inside. I had given up, even though it appeared like I was all in. I wasn't. However, I had someone who could see through my bullshit and tell it like it was. I really needed that, and I hope you have someone who can see you and see through your bullshit too. Someone who can see through the pat replies of "I'm fine" and "I'm okay," all while smiling through the immense pain. That kind of bullshit.

Let me paint the picture for you, because it helped me get to the new.

While I was struggling in my university days and getting ready to be a teacher, I had done neuro-visual optometry and lots of weird eye-brain exercises with a kindhearted, loving practitioner and team. He had had his own personal journey too, and because of this, he could feel that I was deep on mine and whatever transformation was to come from it. After a few months of working together, we decided to stop because I was struggling and hurting (physically and emotionally). The exercises caused me a lot of pain. It hurt every single time to do them. And it was evident that I was emotionally hurting, so he hoped that maybe tending to the feelings was the next step for me.

That hope was the key for anything else to work for me. I'm not sure I was really ready to hear that or believe it, but I can see now that he was right. I was out of hope, and I had a lot of feelings that were vying for my attention and dying to be explored. See how the feelings were a big step in the direction toward where I wanted to go? Naturally, the teacher showed up, and I was ready for more.

Around the time I started seeing the psychotherapist, I got a call from the man who had done the neuro-visual optometry with me. He and his coworkers had recently met a chiropractor who they felt aligned with and really pulled toward connecting with me. This is the "guidance" part. The work he did was more functional neurology, and he specialized in concussions. They pretty much brought me to him without me really wanting to be there. I remember feeling like I should see him because they had put so much effort into making it happen. They had hand-delivered my referral to his office, so being the "perfect" me who always wanted to do the right thing, I went. But I didn't want to.

This chiropractor had a personal tie to brain injuries and was passionate about supporting people with concussions, so they felt like he was a great person for me to see. I imagined it was this chiropractor's own desire for hope that allowed him to have it for me. Rarely do you find someone who truly "gets it" when recovering from a brain injury. But it was in how he spoke to me, how I didn't exactly have to explain my symptoms for him to truly know or understand what I was experiencing that made me feel seen. **Feeling seen is an important step in healing.** We often fear nobody can really see us or understand us when we are dealing with so much on the inside, because it often cannot be seen on the outside.

I feel like I may have gone there kicking and screaming. Or just being really inwardly annoyed, trying to smile and "do my best" at yet another appointment. But I went. I did more baseline testing, more having to talk about my symptoms, and more weird exercises that somehow always involved peppermint oil or funny-colored glasses.

One day he had me read an article from a magazine to test my vision with the weird glasses. I remember picking up the magazine and seeing that, without realizing it, the chiropractor had randomly opened to an article called "The History of Bras." Ah! The hilarity! And just as play is an important part of the healing recipe, so is laughter. It was the first time in a long time that I really laughed. So, we both just sat there laughing while I read aloud about the history of bras. This is an example of being in the old while having an inkling of what's to come. Hint . . . it's about FUN.

Despite my initial resistance, I kept seeing him. He had a beautiful heart, and although I felt discouraged and unsure whether any of this would work, I still tried. I went to see him every week. He felt that my seeing an osteopath would also help. As mentioned early on in this book, I had seen a couple osteopaths along with chiropractors before, so I felt unwilling about whether there was a point, but I listened (more like I did what I was told). I saw the person he wanted me to see, a doctor within his practice. And after telling my story ONE MORE TIME, it turns out she left the practice. So, I saw her, got to know her, felt safe with her and decided to like her, then I couldn't see her anymore. She left, so I had to start over again.

There was a point in that meeting, though. You see, she, too, had been an educator of little ones and had left that job after a health issue and later became an osteopath. That moment with her was part of the healing, and her path had touched mine. Her story helped me find love and acceptance within my own story and journey.

And the teacher who came next was perhaps the one I needed most. Like Michael A. Singer said, situations pop up to "hit your stuff." At this point, I was REALLY resistant to seeing an osteopath, especially after the last one had left. I managed to open up to her because she was a woman—I felt safer to be who I was around another woman, something that was becoming clear. I think prior to my injury, I had a lot of emotional injuries when it came to men, making it hard for me to let them in and trust them—trust that a man could hold me, see me, and show up for me. And that I could let all of me be shared, especially with a person I didn't really know. The raw, the real, the very currently imperfect and messy person that I was, who had up until this point, loved perfection. The part of me that felt "broken" needed to learn how to let someone into the brokenness. That part needed to learn to love all that was there.

So, when the chiropractor told me that the new osteopath he hired was a man, I was even more annoyed. We eventually learn that our teachers cross our path for a reason—and this man turned out to be one of my greatest teachers by being one of the biggest hitters of my shit. This is where we learn to trust who shows up, who we are guided to, even when we want to be the one choosing our teachers. When we pray, we let the Universe show us the way, and sometimes we let go of control and let our soul lead the way. That's what was happening here, even if all I felt was annoyed!

I walked in the office after the broken toe incident (well, more like hobbled in). You see, my toe wouldn't fit into a normal shoe, so I had to borrow a giant sandal from my dad to get to this appointment that I so badly did not want to go to. I hobbled in, with crutches I might add, and I soon found out that this new osteopath was not only a man, but a fairly young one who was closer to my age than what was comfortable for me, seeing as both men and male authority figures were hitters of my shit that I so badly wanted to heal. In other words, they triggered all the shit that needed to be healed. Hence the reason why I was so resistant to letting this support in.

Despite my resistance, he felt weirdly familiar, even though I had never seen him before. The familiarity came from his eyes, gentle and kind, which I think helped ease my stubborn resistance. Additionally, there was a kindness in the way he treated me. His treatments were there to teach me—although I think in some ways, they may have triggered me as well. But both triggers and healing in wholeness are here to reflect to me what I was finally ready to see: the true ME.

It didn't start that way, though. It rarely does, does it?! Recall, I was very annoyed! I know he understood how I felt without my needing to always say it. This made me feel safe and seen. Words were hard for me at that point, which was a barrier to me getting the support I needed and made it that much more frustrating when I had to explain myself over and over again. But being an osteopath, he could feel what I couldn't always say and what other practitioners couldn't see. It felt comforting to finally feel seen (even if it was slightly uncomfortable and made me very vulnerable). As you now know, the symptoms are not always easy to explain, yet osteopaths and most bodyworkers can feel what is going on with you, which is much easier when there is a block between your brain and what you want to say.

And he was kind from the moment he met me and helped me hobble down the stairs to the treatment room. And because this was all about "hitting my shit," naturally, the first question that came out of his mouth was "So what's your story?"

That was the one thing I didn't want to tell anyone one more fucking time! But the story we tell ourselves matters. And it was in that moment that I realized that somewhere along the journey, I had *become* my brain injury. My brain injury had become me, and that was the only story I knew how to tell. And I was sick of telling it. I wanted a new story. I was so much more than this story.

I think he saw that, but I couldn't. At least, not yet. I didn't want my brain injury to be my story anymore, yet I was clinging on to it for dear life, unwilling to fully let go because there was a part of me that was scared it might always be a part of my story. I learned that maybe I needed to let someone in and simply be held in my mess, witnessed in my ongoing journey and its struggles. I needed to allow myself to be held just as I was, imperfect, messy, scared, and unsure. He held me in a way that allowed me to let go, to feel like I no longer needed to do this journey on my own. With him, I learned to trust that someone else could hold me while I found my way, that it was safe to trust my team of practitioners and allow them to care for me emotionally as I navigated this journey. It was safe to receive the care and expertise I needed to heal. I'm not sure I had ever fully felt that way before.

The thing about "feeling held" is that I also learned how extremely healing touch can be. Osteopathy is a very hands-on healing modality, much like massage therapy, acupuncture, or physiotherapy and chiropractic work. And truth be told, I hadn't really let myself be touched in a while.

I remember wanting to turn off my emotions every week when I went to see him. In all honesty, I felt pretty awkward, like I didn't have much to say. It was hard at first because I had a lot of triggers—off-limits topics—that didn't help my nervous system. They sometimes sent me into a shame spiral of the "not enough" feelings that were so ready to "be hit" and be loved. Even in those challenging moments when I wanted to close myself off emotionally, there was a little voice within that would remind me to "stay open." So, I did, not just with him, but with all the practitioners who were by my side and on my team. In the moments of resistance, I was reminded to simply STAY OPEN. That's an important step that can help us when we are the most scared and unwilling.

We must stay open to what these people have to teach us. There is something that Bernie Siegel calls the "healing partnership." In his book *Love, Medicine & Miracles,* he talks about healing in a very different way than I knew. Siegel beautifully describes the patient-practitioner partnership and what this is all about. These people were my partners on my healing journey. They were learning and healing alongside me. They were no longer the people who were in control or holding power over me, but they were sitting on the sidelines, learning, experimenting, trying and falling down and getting back up WITH ME.

The teachers I was guided to were no longer the kind that I was guided to before, early on in my journey. They were not there to fix me or heal me in the ways I had been. They were there to see me, to support me, to learn alongside me, and to guide me back home to *me*. They saw me when I couldn't see myself. That vision of me in my wholeness, of what was ahead for me even when I saw blank. It's like the song "I Can See Clearly Now." Although I was still stuck in the storm, the pain and the path forward continued to get clearer as we navigated it together. The missing ingredients kept showing up alongside them—yet so did the moments when I continued to keep my foot stuck in the old, in the familiar, in the safety of what I knew.

I want to explain what I mean. Osteopathy is all about seeing a patient as a whole, and the difference with these practitioners was that they saw all of me: all of Amanda. They didn't only see "the brain-injured Amanda," the Amanda with all the symptoms. They saw beyond that, and they wanted to allow me to see it too.

All the while I was learning to see, love, and accept all parts of me, I continued to hold onto this fear story of "What if this is where I stay? What if I really have plateaued? What if there isn't another way?"

I was still stuck. And as much as I was finally in a more loving place within myself, I was still unsure of whether I would ever feel better and fully heal. With all these people by my side, I was a little bit like Humpty Dumpty. All the osteopaths, chiropractors, naturopaths, homeopaths, brain specialists (and more) couldn't put Amanda back together again. But the thing was, I wasn't Humpty Dumpty, and the point of the journey wasn't exactly to put me back together again. It was to love and accept all the pieces that felt the most broken, the most misaligned, and the most human while finding me underneath it all. There was a "me" underneath that wanted to be freed. Unleashed, accepted, unapologetically being me. The journey and the teachers were the exact steps I needed to find *her*—the real *me*.

And the beautiful thing is that every person, every next step was there to help me heal myself and find the *me* that was there all along. To help me let go of the label, the perfect patient, the rulebook, and the worry that I may never get better. They were holding me in this vision of the new while we still were a little stuck in this past pattern and uncertainty of whether the new was even possible.

Despite this, **they did teach me that I was not a patient who needed to be fixed, but rather a person to be loved.** I felt love, true self-love.

Even though our appointments were often geared around what to do, what to try next, and on fixing or managing the symptoms, the real lessons came from the love and care they gave to me, and the way they made me feel: finally seen and no longer alone. In a way, they helped me believe again—one day, one shared moment, and one appointment at a time.

I didn't need more medications, protocols, or practitioners telling me what to do; I needed loving compassion from another human being and a reminder of what was truly possible when I had lost this.

So, let's get back to that important ingredient in the recipe of healing: holding onto the feeling and belief of what's possible. And being in a place to receive and fully accept it.

Let your teachers come to you and guide you back to your belief. Sometimes we are guided to the teachers, the partners, and the healers who can hold the vision of us in our wholeness until we can hold it for ourselves. When we forget who we are, we need someone to remind us. When we have lost hope, we need the people who can hold out for the hope of what can be until we are ready to feel and believe in it for ourselves.

Bernie Siegel talks about how "hope is not just practical, it is physiological." Believing in something actually creates it. **The mind's belief that the body can heal literally creates those physiological changes.** We can't solely focus on the body and ignore the mind. They are intertwined. When they are on the same page, our bodies can heal. But sometimes when we are focusing so hard on fixing or healing the body, the opposite happens. Our mind gets in the way, and our lack of belief holds us back from achieving what we most desire. Our bodies feel like a problem to be fixed rather than something that is doing its best and knows what to do! Our doubt keeps us in a state of dissonance, and even though our actions (doing all the right things to heal) are there, if we do not fully believe, our body continues to mirror that reality to us, and as a result, it stays stuck in the belief that we are sick.

My faith and belief in myself and my ability to get better was the missing ingredient. My fear of "what if the person who told me I cannot heal is right and I might never be able to" was holding me hostage in the past, in the pain, in being the sick person. As a result, my body and I continued to play that role, and this meant never letting myself wholeheartedly believe in what could be—what was possible.

That's when my next teachers appeared and taught me about the mindbody connection, introducing me to the concept of **neuroplasticity** and the brain/body's ability to heal itself with belief. It's kind of like the placebo effect.

In Siegel's book he states, "Science teaches that we must see in order to believe, but we must also believe in order to see. We must be receptive to possibilities that science has not yet grasped, or we will miss them."

This claim makes sense, and it also *feels* like magic. This is what we needed as a team: to surrender to the possibilities that we had never tried or known before. To open up to limitless possibilities . . . to find belief in a time when we had tried just about everything, and when belief was the main ingredient missing.

So, let's stay open because what comes next is the piece of the puzzle that you might never have seen coming, the piece that is meant for you. Let the teacher come your way, and don't forget to welcome the weird, synchronistic, and magical ways in which your next step, your next puzzle piece, and your next miracles arrive.

TAKEAWAY & P L A Y

Time to journal and reflect. Feel free to take these one at a time, and give yourself all the time, space, and grace you need.

- What are you learning from the teachers in your life?
- What are they guiding you to?
- How are they guiding you home to the real *you*?
- What "stories" are you ready to let go of?
- What is the thing keeping you stuck in the past, unwilling to fully put both feet into what you truly desire?
- What is the underlying fear, the "story" that might be getting in the way?
- What kind of teachers have come your way?
- What are they teaching you?
- Can you let them hold you? Can you let them see you fully? Can you let them help you see the real you?
- Most importantly, what shit has been hit that wants to let love, acceptance, and HOPE into it? (**This is the breakthrough, even if it feels like a breakdown!**)
- And if you haven't had this yet, what kind of teachers or partners do you desire to invite into your life, your journey, and into your heart?
- Can you stay OPEN? Are you willing to open your heart, especially when it wants to close?

TAKEAWAY &

Set the intention now.

Describe the person or people you want to have by your side.

How do you **FEEL** when you are in their presence? What do they help you to see, to know, to feel, and to believe just by having them in your life?

Let yourself feel into the possibility of what's to come and trust that it is perfectly on time. Let yourself receive the breadcrumbs.

Chapter 9

THE POWER OF COLLECTIVE HEALING

Remember the weird breadcrumbs that will guide you on your path—have you noticed any?

No? Perhaps you're feeling annoyed, lost, and still stuck in your mud? Don't worry if that's where you are. **There's something good coming—I can attest to that.** And believing that only good things can come your way, no matter what, will make it so.

I am reminded that sometimes our darkest moments can occur right before we experience any sort of breakthrough. So, if it's dark right now, stay with me a little longer. This part won't last forever.

Right now you may feel like nothing is different. Yet you have asked for all the support—the lessons and the miracles. You have shown up and continue to show up for it all (the feelings, the teachers, the learning, the "trying all the things") and still feel like nothing is working. The shifts don't seem to occur as fast as the trauma did. You still aren't "better" or where you desire to be. However, your hope and faith are likely higher than they've ever been because of the support in your life. And part of you feels like the more focus you put on healing, the more you continue to get diagnosed with illnesses. Your body seems to wear your symptoms loud and proud—instead of releasing that identity you so badly desire to shift. And it makes no sense at all, especially when you are so focused on your recovery, healing, and doing all the right things.

This feels like the opposite of what you asked and prayed for. I get it. At this point in my journey, I felt a little like Pokémon—"Gotta Catch 'Em All"—when it came to collecting more and more illnesses, diagnoses, viruses, or protocols, and it didn't feel FUN at all! Yet I knew there had to be a reason for it.

Our road to believing, healing, and coming home to ourselves will be full of moments and pit stops that make absolutely no sense. Yet trust that these detours are there for a reason, for a season. And you will be led to your moments, your breadcrumbs, your rainbow.

I'm here to remind you that even in these moments there is a rainbow (clarity) coming your way. It will be this or something better beyond this. Don't give up hope now! You've come such a long way. Your hope is the one thing that has been getting you through, allowing you to dive wholeheartedly into the new, into the possibilities, and into your future full of heart, hope, and dreams to come true. Cheesy, I know, but I see you, and I am not letting you give up on your dreams or even dreaming about your possibilities.

I, too, was in the dark. This darkness came right before the biggest breadcrumb came my way. But looking back, there were several breadcrumbs before this moment that led me to say YES to this new program and way of being. Recall in the last chapter how the biggest things I needed were belief and to support my mind by allowing my body to heal.

What led me to this—to say YES to a new way of being? Quite a lot!

Enter one of my very first breadcrumbs, Dr. Norman Doidge. I first heard about him from my roommate in university, then once again when I was deep on my healing journey—the part of it where I was ALL IN and ready to do whatever it took. That's when I finally picked up his book *The Brain's Way of Healing*. **It opened me up to the idea that although the brain could get stuck in a pattern that was unhelpful, it was possible to rewire the brain to change and heal on its own.**

Doidge was my first introduction to neuroplasticity, which completely countered the "I had plateaued and wouldn't get better" idea. It expanded my belief in what's possible, and that is what we need most when it's kind of dark. We need examples that expand our consciousness and belief in what can be. My friend calls these "expanders."

And back to the science part of things. **Neuroplasticity is the idea that the brain can heal itself.** The brain is literally like plastic—malleable, moldable, and flexible. The brain CAN change and is not stuck, unlike the fearful belief I had been hanging on to.

Then came my naturopath's insightful suggestion to check out Dr. Joe Dispenza's books on the mind-body connection to healing. His books, particularly *You Are the Placebo*, were super helpful to me in cementing my new beliefs around what was possible. He came a while after this next breadcrumb did. They were connected because they were a big part of the hope that slowly took up more space in my heart where worry was once a permanent resident. Something happened whenever I remembered all the breadcrumbs, all the helpers, all the moments when it felt dark before the next step appeared. This was hope in action. All the teachers and the stories were proof of what was possible. You see, sometimes, when we are living in doubt, we need proof upon proof and story upon story of what's possible to reinforce a new belief and a new way.

This is one of those moments when the light turns on in the dark. I want you to know where I was because it was indeed dark again. But my beliefs were getting stronger, even in the dark. This time it was like an arrow being pulled backward before shooting forward. It was about to get really good. But first it felt really bad.

This was a day when I felt like shit and just wished that things were different. I was deeply in need of the shift. My mom's side of the family was hosting a reunion with her cousins and extended family from the United States, people we hadn't seen in forever. Dinner at a restaurant was the plan—a plan that proved to be a huge challenge for me. It was something so simple, yet the mere thought and anticipation of having dinner in a restaurant was filled with triggers and induced a lot of pain and fear for me. I had grown to become terrified of the simplest things like lights, noise, people, food, and all my anxiety about them just worsened my response.

Before going, my mom needed to check the menu to make sure I would be able to eat something with my limited diet (and most recent diet suggestions). But that was the least of my fears. I was more afraid of being in the room with all these people—them asking about me and my current life and illness—plus all that noise and light. There would be too much stimulation, and I'd been doing my best to avoid or limit these triggers in hope of getting better. At that time, people, noise, and light made my head hurt more than ever, and my feeling like a broken failure whenever anyone asked me how I was doing didn't help much either. Putting attention on making the symptoms go away and being a permanent patient doing everything to make things get better was actually creating an unwanted response.

So, there I was at this family reunion, miserable and overstimulated and feeling like I couldn't stay another minute or add any value to the conversation. I was severely challenged in this environment, and I couldn't simply be there. So, I excused myself so I could walk the streets to get some relief. I was in so much pain, and underneath all of it, I felt sad, even more depressed, misunderstood, deeply alone, and unsure whether I would ever get better at the current rate I was going. From where I saw it, I was getting worse, not better.

And that's when the next breadcrumb appeared, because sometimes they arrive in the strangest ways, when we least expect them, and when we most need them.

That family reunion gave my mom and her cousins the chance to connect and to share about their lives and what had been going on for them. Naturally, my mom's story included me, my journey, and my struggles.

Upon hearing about my story, my mom's cousin thought of someone she knew who had had a similar journey navigating many illnesses and who had used all of the similar healing modalities and supplements to help. This woman went to a program and was now completely healed. She was no longer on any supplements or protocols. Wow!

Her story sounded too good to be true. I thought to myself, *Okay, but she didn't have a brain injury.*

We tend to do that, to dismiss a positive example. "Yes, that's great for her, but her story and journey aren't exactly like mine. So, how can I trust that it will work for me?"

Despite this, I listened to the suggestion to connect with this woman and hear her story. I now understand that sometimes just hearing someone else's journey is the exact healing and next step we may need. The breadcrumbs remind us that something we are afraid may never happen for us is indeed possible. So, I gave her my number and waited for the call.

I remember being anxious when the call came, not knowing what to say, what to share, or what to ask. But I didn't have to worry because once she began sharing her story, I just knew. Something in my thinking and belief changed that day. I wanted to know more. I had this feeling, like a tingle in my head, that there was something there, and I was about to find out what. The tingling sensation was unlike the pain I was used to. It kept coming whenever I was headed in the direction of something new, as if something new was wiring and finding a way through my brain. Maybe it was a little hint of what was to come!

It was weird, but it felt quite magical as if I was headed in the right direction. So, whenever I felt the tingle, I followed it. Interestingly enough, it would only make its presence known when I was really in the moment, listening to a song I loved or spending time with a little one near and dear to my heart. You know, the moments I was fully present in the moment and not in the stress, the mess, or the sickness, which was doing the opposite of fixing, finding solutions, and trying anything and everything.

It came when I stopped doing and started being, and that's where we were headed, but together this time. Sometimes the biggest change happens when we connect with others who are in need of the same medicine and magic we are. There's something powerful in collective intention and connection. It brings us in a new and more loving direction.

In the moments I felt this tingly feeling, I felt like something was there *for* me and *beyond* me. I trusted that feeling now and the fact that these people were there to help me rewire the fear and wholeheartedly believe in and create a new story.

But let's start with the fear—you know, the fear that although this woman got better, I might not. What helped me with this fear was hearing her share that there were other people with concussions and brain injuries who went to the same program she did. The part of my subconscious that needed to hear this helped me expand to a greater understanding.

I then learned that most trauma is actually a brain injury (whether or not it is referred to in that way). So, when someone goes through a lot of stress or a traumatic experience like loss, an accident, witnessing something frightening, or experiencing a lot of transitions in a short amount of time, such as living in the many changes, restrictions, and sickness/loss experienced in the past few years with COVID-19, changes in the brain occur.

With COVID, everything from parenting with the added stressors and time at home together, isolation and avoidance practices and increased loneliness, and lack of sufficient childcare or mental health support can all be contributors to experiencing heightened stress and a trauma response in the brain/nervous system. This in and of itself can be trauma, which is an injury to the brain, ultimately changing how the brain is wired. (So, if up until now you hadn't recognized how this book could support you, know that if you're a human navigating COVID, there is a chance your wiring has shifted a little bit and the tools, stories, and new patterns to be created through this book can help you too!)

As I said, the brain is affected when there is trauma; a part of our brain known as the limbic system goes on high alert. It's the part of our brain that creates feelings. Our feelings are important, and it turns out that when we have a heightened emotional response associated with trauma or a bunch of challenges, our limbic system can get mixed up, even when there is a small trigger. This trigger reminds you of what once happened, and your body prepares to cope with it as if it is happening again. It's fight or flight in action. The body's way to protect itself is the exact thing that stops us from healing, feeling healthy, and whole-heartedly moving forward. Because on a subconscious level, we keep expecting that what once happened to us—our mud, our rock bottom moment—is going to happen again.

Constant states of ongoing stress or addiction to feelings like depression, anxiety or fear, and sadness can cause our brain (our limbic system) to stay stuck in this state and have trouble moving through it. That's why after some big change, trauma, or experience that places us in a powerless state, we can get stuck there because our brain is still stuck there! This heightened response in the limbic system is called "over-firing," and even the slightest amount of stress causes this part of the brain to scream, "Danger! Danger!"

When a symptom-trigger or something from the past that was slightly or acutely stressful comes up, our brain starts screaming, "THIS IS NOT SAFE!"

Safety is a whole lot more than a roof over our head, something that became clear when I was interviewed to see if the program this woman recommended would be a good fit for me. I picked up the phone to chat with someone from the program's team, knowing very little about it at the time. The questions they asked prompted some aha moments, but I'll be honest, it didn't start out that way. Remember that feeling of want-ing to run and hide (a.k.a. the fight-or-flight response)? Well, my brain and body felt like that while on that call, as I was asked very personal questions. I was triggered in the "let's see if I'm a good fit for it" call.

This response in itself made it clear that it was the exact program I needed because I hadn't heard of or given any thought to the limbic system, and it was at the forefront of what was going on in my brain.

Something about the questions they asked just brought me into this deep inner knowing that despite the safety net of home and other material things being there in my life, I had never felt safe inside. My constant fight-or-flight response was because my limbic system was overfiring and wired in a way that kept this loop going. This created the maladaptive stress response, which is really what was behind all that wanting to "run and hide."

The aha that came from this knowledge was understanding that growing up as a sensitive kid, having a pretty reactive nervous system and limbic system, followed by the accident that occurred later on in life, which resulted in emotional, physical, and physiological changes, was like the perfect storm. The combination of all this stress and trauma made it hard to get out of that pattern and habitual response. Thus, it was clear that something new was needed to create new loops in the brain that were wired for happiness, health, and love as opposed to the constant loops of fear, anxiety, and needing to protect myself from all the things that triggered pain!

Early on in this book I mentioned that I had always felt, even from a young age, that I had this incessant need to maintain control in every situation; I had to make others feel good in order to feel safe in my own body, my own being, in my own world. Feeling wholeheartedly safe on the inside, to me, meant managing my outer surroundings.

It was a lot of pressure that constantly activated those fight-or-flight feelings, which made it hard to feel safe or let my body do what it's designed to do: heal and activate what is known as the parasympathetic nervous system, the part of our nervous system that allows our body to rest, digest, and repair, and helps homeostasis come into place!

When we never feel safe, our body doesn't know how to do what it is naturally designed to do. Our adrenaline spikes along with our cortisol whenever we are triggered with anything big or small or when we are experiencing an emotional response or a big feeling or symptom. We feel like we're running from a tiger or readying ourselves to fight back.

This phone call made me profoundly aware of this information, and I just remember feeling stuck. I always thought I had felt safe. Yet even though I said yes when the person on the phone asked if I felt safe as a child, my tears made it very clear that the truth was a big, resounding no. Especially because I had been an empathic, sensitive child who felt everything, my limbic system must have been overstimulated A LOT, hence why it wasn't so easy to acknowledge it. My tears said more than my words, just like they had when I was a sensitive little kiddo!

Perhaps there was a link here between my childhood, my limbic system, and my brain's response to the brain injury and other "traumas." Maybe there was a perfect storm that kept my brain stuck in this loop, unable to discern danger from everyday stressors. And constantly focusing on these symptoms and trying to find solutions to the problems only reinforced this loop, thus making it hard for my body to heal itself.

I knew that day on that phone call that I was indeed a perfect fit for this program. To me, allowing myself to receive this kind of support not only made sense but was also the answer to bypassing the triggers and focusing on the way I wanted to feel. What often happens in healing is that doctors and specialists constantly "check in" on the symptoms. For instance, "Are they getting better or worse?" or "What triggers them or makes them go away?" rather than focusing on changing the mechanism that alters the response. Or better yet, focusing wholeheartedly on the response and feeling you actually want to create rather than focusing on what you want to get away from.

Finding out about the program was an incredibly important breadcrumb—the one that would change my whole way of healing; the one I needed in order to get my life back, or better yet, create the one I truly wanted.

Sometimes we feel like if we focus on what we don't want right now, maybe it will prevent us from experiencing it later. But worrying about the future is like suffering twice. When we worry in the present, we experience the punishment now because we somehow think it will make it better later on because we saw it coming. We feel like we can avoid that "I told you so" feeling. But when we do that, we miss the opportunity to find peace in the present or fully acknowledge our real feelings and fears. I spent most of my days in fear or worry about what would happen if I went outside of my safety zone and comfort zone—knowing that doing so would bring more suffering and symptoms. Constantly living in fear and worry reinforced the story of living in fear, and I constantly questioned and second-guessed my abilities—what could I do, what couldn't I do, where could I go, where couldn't I go. It was time to shift this way of being!

I was scared that I wouldn't make it through the program, mostly because being around people was HARD. My concentration/focus was again "one thing per day," and afterward I required rest, a nap, or time alone. Yet this program was five full days of people (ALL DAY LONG) and not sleeping in my own bed or having my very predictable "routines" that helped me feel good (or as good as I could).

Still, my heart knew it was the thing I needed. So, despite the resistance rising in me, I said yes. My parents supported my choice to go, even though we had already spent SO MUCH money, time, and energy on so many things. We all shared a collective feeling that this program was different, that this program was the missing piece of the puzzle that we had never learned about until now. Better late than never, I thought.

And once I fully opened myself to receiving this help, more seren-dipities followed shortly after I applied to the program. As the Universe would have it, the next five-day in-person seminar program was actually taking place in the town I had yet to go back to: the one where I had hit my rock bottom while still in my teaching job, the one I chose to leave because I felt inexplicably sad, broken, depressed, and embar-rassed. This felt like a sign that there was something there, begging to be unearthed and healed. Yes, this pit of mud was something I hadn't yet sat through, and I felt maybe it was now time to be there (amid the weird sign of needing to go back)! November came, and I showed up, uncertain of what the week would bring and with a heart full of hope (and yes, still a fair bit of resistance and fear).

Just like everyone I had been guided to in the past, the person who created this program did so because of her own need for healing, for hope, for a miracle. She had a miraculous healing journey and birthed an incredible five-day program and online video program as a result so she could help others undergoing the same. Her program helped me shift my beliefs and see myself in a new light. It started out as needing to learn how to calm the storm within and bloomed into feeling the power we all have to create our own miracle and our life beyond the limitations we have. She also guided me to understanding the magic of mirror neurons—of new beginnings and mostly, of DREAMING again.

This week showed me the power of coming together with a powerful vision and feeling the magic of what's possible. It was similar to Dr. Joe Dispenza's journey, where he healed himself through holding a clear vision of himself as well, healthy, and with an aligned spine and by being surrounded by loving support and feeling elevated emotions like joy, love, gratitude, and so on. I think all group programs are like that.

When we are in a group, the possibilities are endless and the experiences are amplified. There was so much power in sharing this experience and healing in a group. Because of this, we got to witness one another heal and transcend our symptoms in what felt like MIRACULOUS and MAGICAL ways. It was clear for me that being in a program like this was the way forward, holding these collective intentions together.

We were asked at the beginning of the program to stop referring to our sickness and our labels (anything outside of who we are as people). For the first time, I felt like a person who could connect with others and be with them without fear. I felt like I could finally be myself with understanding, with hope, and with connection. I also got to connect with parts of myself I had not had the chance to in a really LONG time. I remember the moment I knew this was the medicine I needed. It was the moment I realized through this journey of healing that somewhere along the way, I had stopped dreaming.

This method of healing is focused on the FUTURE: living as if it is already here and embodying that feeling within before experiencing it in the real world. Living in the possibility of what's to come while feeling how you want to feel in the present moment. If you are currently sick and have not been able to travel or have a partner or family of your own or go somewhere because of limitations, then your job isn't to seek the triggers and dissect them, but it's to live as if you are experiencing these shifts now.

There is a lot more to this, but *this* is the part you need to know. This is the part *I* needed to know. That for someone who has powerful feelings (and can limit her life with the state of her limbic system), I could become limitless by tapping into these magical feelings and the powers they held. That instead of succumbing to feelings of hopelessness, despair, and shame every single day, I could use feelings such as hope, love, joy, play, fun, and more to alter my nervous system's response and to find a way forward by believing that I am living that future RIGHT NOW.

The first day of the program, I was asked the question, "So, Amanda, where are you going to travel to first when you are better?" It was such a simple question, yet I had no answer. I had been afraid to "go there," to find hope or to believe that a different future was possible because "what if it never happened?"

This was my big aha moment. I had been placing so much energy on finding answers that allowed for the life I wanted. But I couldn't cultivate the sense of safety I desired or the wholehearted belief that I could ever actually have that life. I needed to dream again and believe in what could be. **I needed to believe in possibilities more than limitations.**

And it turns out the heart had everything to do with it. Rather than healing my body with my brain, it was time to come back to my heart.

As a client recently put it, "The loop came into my heart."

When the triggers, the stress, the symptoms appear, it's time to tap into the heart, the dream, the vision beyond this current hiccup. Whenever thoughts such as *When will this feeling, symptom, or sickness go away?* or *Why me?* appeared, I released the need to find the reasons why and chose to move into possibilities instead. I could accept what emotions or fears were up for me and then intentionally direct my thoughts into feeling all the possibilities beyond the present moment or the present circumstance. I created new thoughts, patterns, and realities through believing and feeling my way toward them.

It was time to wholeheartedly BELIEVE and hold onto that feeling because this is the perfect manifesting recipe to a life well lived and a brain/body well healed. But my journey was long and not always smooth—and I have learned a lot since then . . . mostly about what works for me and this may work for you!

So, I want to make it easier for you than it was for me. There were many steps and some rules involved and some places I got a bit "stuck" again, so I'm going to highlight what really resonated with me (leading with my heart). Your heart knows what it wants (and also what it's scared may never come to be). So, allow your heart's magic to do its thing, and start with one dream, one vision, and one heart full of FEELING at a time!

But that's not the only important part of this step. The collective healing and dreaming was the ultimate game changer for me. This is where the mirror neurons come in. There's power in sharing with others. It's one thing to daydream, visualize, or imagine what you want on your own, but it's even more powerful when you share it with someone who believes in it just as much or even more than you do while letting yourself claim it out loud and proud!

The phenomenon of mirror neurons is like a chain reaction: when I feel, you feel! We take on each other's emotions, energies, and more, which is why who you surround yourself with as part of your support system on this journey is incredibly important. When I heal, you heal. Cue collective dance parties and sing-alongs. Happy hormones, get ready!

When one person shares their story or their vision while feeling these heightened emotions, our neurons and brain respond to match and mirror them. For example, if I listen to someone tell me about this amazing date they had where they felt so loved and seen and giddy, my brain thinks this same experience is happening for me and I, too, respond with feeling loved, seen, and giddy. These exact neuro-chemicals in my brain are elicited like oxytocin (a.k.a. the love drug). It's also the same reason why when we watch a movie, we feel what the characters feel. That's why watching a romantic comedy can make you feel all ooey-gooey and love-filled, while watching a violent movie can elicit that same feeling of anger or fear. These are mirror neurons at play.

So, with this new awareness, choose how you want to use the wisdom of mirror neurons to play with the possibilities for your life and your future. Choose who and what you want to surround yourself with because what they show you and share with you allows your brain to match it, which in turn helps you shift your reality and your brain.

Thus, when someone tells me what shift or new experience happened for them, my brain actually thinks I am already having the experience. Whoa! This makes it so much easier to have that experience for myself and for my brain to get on board.

Let's keep sharing our visions, our wins, our big dreams, and the futures we want to create for ourselves. When we share in it together, it speeds up the process, and together, we rise.

Together is always better.

TAKEAWAY & P L A Y

We are going to dream again.

But be gentle with yourself as you use your dreaming muscles for the first time in a while. It's time to strengthen and reinforce dreaming in real time, but start small, slow, and steady.

Don't go with the biggest dream just yet. That one will come. Maybe we start off with a place you haven't been able to go to lately or with a friend you haven't connected with in a while. Or by watching a movie you have always wanted to see but couldn't because it didn't feel good before. Or going on a coffee date by yourself or with a friend or someone special. Or finally enjoying a yummy food that used to cause you symptoms. Or maybe you see yourself at your favorite park or nature spot, feeling energetic and skipping through the forest. Or getting cozy under the blankets by the fire while reading your favorite book, which feels easy to read and more enjoyable than ever before.

Whatever it is, let yourself feel into the possibility as if you are doing it right here, right now.

Feel those feelings wash over you, one moment at a time. Trust me, this works.

I want you to start practicing and living it now.

TAKEAWAY & PLAY

Stop focusing on the limitations or placing limits on what you can't do and start focusing on what you currently can do while letting this list expand! We get to celebrate every win and step (and dream) in the direction of where we choose to go.

Your PLAY for this chapter is to:

1. Take a big piece of paper and start drawing on or decorating it. It's vision board time but DREAM STYLE.

*   Where do you see yourself?
*   Who is with you?
*   What are you doing?
*   How do you FEEL? Here's an example: Draw a picture of yourself sitting on the beach with a lover by your side, feeling whole, worthy, loved and adored, being able to go wherever the heck you want, whenever you desire, and feeling so freaking good! Or draw a vision of yourself being at a friend's party and keeping up with conversations, dancing the night away, and having the best time with your buds. Or draw yourself in a career you LOVE! Remember: It's your dream, so you CHOOSE! Make it fun, whatever you do!

TAKEAWAY & P L A Y

2. Put on your favorite songs, sing or dance along, and embrace this feeling right now.

- How do you feel when you're in this moment, not thinking, just being and living in joy?
- Let yourself lean further into this joy while letting this vibration guide you to dream when you feel ready. Don't rush. Allow your mind to get on board after your heart feels a little better, a little fuller.

The idea behind this exercise is to borrow the feeling from the music until your mirror neurons help you feel it yourself. When we shift into feelings and emotions of higher vibrations (joy, love, play, silliness, and so on), it's much easier to start and keep dreaming because our belief is much higher than when we are staying in fear. Whenever we stay stuck in lower energetic vibrations, we have trouble feeling excited about the possibilities. So, get excited first, get into the feeling, find the FUN, then DREAM.

TAKEAWAY & PLAY

3. Read things, watch things, or dream about things you are not yet able to do, are ready to start doing, or desire to experience one day. We like social proof. Our brains and nervous systems want to know it's possible for us. Watching a video, reading a book, or listening to someone's story of their life or what they have overcome (when it's what we want or are moving toward) also teaches us that we can have it too. It shows us what's possible for us.

Mirror neurons help our brain create these neural shifts, thinking that their experience is ours! Yay for this! Let's keep seeing this as a gift and letting it get us there faster.

Chapter 10

LOVE IS MY SUPERPOWER.
WHAT'S YOURS?

No problem can be solved by the same level of consciousness that created it.

–Albert Einstein

We've talked a lot about "rewiring" the brain, which is part of what we are doing here. But sometimes the path we start on isn't the one we need to take. Although it was neuroplasticity we were experiencing, what resonated for me was the true power of the heart. For someone who was less "science-minded" and more emotion-focused, this is what landed for me and made it all the easier for me to make these changes in both my brain and my body.

Sometimes we find an entry point to the *heart* of the matter that we didn't know was the way through. See what I did there?! When we get stuck in our head, our heart is the next best place to go. Maybe this is indeed another point of the journey.

When we try to heal ourselves by using our logic or rationale—healing the brain by using the brain—we tend to get stuck. We keep the trauma and fear loop going round and round, just like a merry-go-round. It's like that scene in *Grey's Anatomy* when Meredith's mom is at the carousel and she keeps saying, "It's terrible, honey, the carousel never stops spinning. It just keeps going and going."

We've been there, done that, and we're now ready to get off that carousel and find a new loop. We want to stop the spinning, the "merry-go-round" thoughts, feelings, and illnesses that keep us stuck in our current reality. We need to finally get beyond it.

So, let's first take a deep breath, in and out. Inhale the new, exhale the old. Breathe in, let go, and breathe it all back into our hearts. The heart can handle whatever we are ready to release. Our heart has our back. So, breathe into that heart. This is where we will start.

Sometimes we need to find a different route to our healing, and getting out of the brain (this constant loop) and into the heart seems to be the way through. Finding love and feeling it in those moments actually creates a new loop.

When I first learned to meditate, my pain (or energy) would get stuck in my head. As it turns out, there was a reason for it. Maybe I had been stuck in my head my whole life and this was my chance to finally live in and from my heart. Well, at least this was my chance to do my best to spend more time there than in my head.

I don't think it's a coincidence that a major symptom for me was pain in my head. Migraines might just be a medical message that we're living in our head—in our worries and our fears more than we are in our hearts. For me, I had been living in my head my whole life. I had been thinking through everything rather than feeling through things, including my recovery. Maybe the uncovering or unlearning was a way for me to get back to me, and who I am is love. Who I am *is* someone who lives in and from her heart. **We all are.** Somewhere over time we forgot to be who we are—an embodiment of love for ourselves and others. We are unable to remember this truth because no one around us modeled this way of living to us because they, too, never got a chance to remember. So, maybe this brain injury really was a gift in a weird and painful package. Maybe this was my chance to learn to love more and to finally start living through my heart—to wear my emotions on my sleeve, to be who I am without holding anything back, and to let love guide me home to my true unconditionally loving self.

Here's where it all changed for me: We've heard about dreaming, about focusing on how you want to feel and what your future looks like, feels like, and is imagined like. I have a big poster in my room that has quotes on it, one being *My inspiration is my imagination.* This is true, and **the ingredients are imagination + heart.** Our power lies in feeling the depth of our emotions. The biggest thing I learned was how much our feelings influence our reality.

Our predominant feelings toward anyone, including ourselves, influence the types of experiences we invite into our lives. Our feelings are a frequency in our heart. Our hearts are powerful and send out electrical messages. Much like trying to tune into your favorite radio station while driving down rural roads, if the frequency of our heart is weak, cloudy, and muddy (because we haven't actually taken time to sit with our mud yet), we will have trouble attracting and feeling into experiences that are a full-body yes for us—those filled with love, fun, silliness, joy, and all the good vibrations! For example, when you feel sad, more sadness seems to come your way; much like a magnet, it somehow seems to find you. Likewise, when something really good happens, we inevitably feel happy, and it is that feeling of happiness that tends to attract more experiences that make us feel happy.

Our feelings and our energetic vibrations are contagious. Much like the theory of mirror neurons, our feelings are magnets for other people having the same feelings and experiences. Like attracts like, feelings attract feelings, and LOVE attracts LOVE. Our heart sends out an electromagnetic message, which then leads us to find and receive our energetic match.

Warning: It isn't always as straightforward as that. Sometimes, feeling your sadness by loving yourself enough to feel is actually being in the love frequency.

So, don't stop feeling those FEELS—yes, I'm talking about sadness and being in the depths of your lower emotions. It's okay and safe to feel them fully and to love yourself through that process without placing a "good" or "bad" label on any feeling.

Sometimes when you are truly living from your heart and being heart-centered in your interactions with others, as an empath, you might attract people who are drawn to you for that exact reason. And unless you have the capacity and energetic boundary to not take on their emotions, you might feel depleted. So, this is something we will feel our feelings around too, because when we are in a state of feeling "bad," we just need to let that be heard, loved on, and not judged. Compassion is our compass yet again. We need it and so do others in our lives.

The key here is that no feeling is bad. Yet all feelings are powerful. Let's make it safe to sit with and be friends with our feelings while tapping into their wisdom and power. There is no need to run from the sad, the mad, or the other feelings that don't feel good. Sit with them, listen to them, breathe through them and with them, and then come back to your heart. Let's "make friends with them," then consciously amplify the ones that we DO want more of! Allow yourself to let the feelings be okay so you can shift into also knowing their power, thus using it for good!

Think of yourself as a superhero who has superpowers (feelings). Stay with me here. We will dive deeply into this idea and why we get to choose our superpowers and use our sensitivity to finally be our best friend and our biggest power! Like Pikachu, we get to choose which Pokémon we want to be and what our powers are used for. Rather than needing to collect them all unconsciously, we are instead all capable of choosing and using them wisely.

We have the power to allow our feelings to define us or to empower us. Realizing how sensitive I have always been means that I feel A LOT. Any feeling I feel is big and intense, something that can either be seen as a negative or as a blessing. I was about to find out how this sensitivity could finally feel like a blessing. It was time to redefine my sensitivity and heart as my superpower. The thing that made me sicker is also the thing that would make me better, and not just better, but happier, healthier, and more loving than ever.

It was in this moment that I finally realized that I could use my innately given ability to feel, to heal! One of the things about me (and likely about you too) is that I could get myself into any state of being and feeling in a matter of seconds and feel that feeling within every part of me. Happiness was a full-body feeling, and so was sadness, fear, and hopelessness. And love. Oh LOVE, did I ever feel that feeling all over when I let myself.

This is where we Sensitive Sallys find the power that lies within us and where we stop looking outside of ourselves for safety. Yet, our sensitive superpowers are why we didn't feel so safe in the first place. It's the reason why we mastered "Pokémon-ing" our way through sicknesses.

It's exactly why what started out on a healing journey ended up in manifesting more labels, illnesses, and symptoms. When we ignite a feeling mixed with an intention, we are incredibly gifted at getting exactly what we feel and imagine! We are magical manifesting unicorns! So, fixating on fear (feeling) mixed with sickness (focusing on the thing we don't want) ends up creating the recipe for exactly what we do not want in the first place: more sickness (and consequently, more fear).

I learned this the hard way. It's not meant to scare you but to help you not be as frightened as I was and to comfort you through any fears you may have alongside the hope you may have too. This story and chapter will guide you to focus on the power of your heart. Every time you focus on that fear—the thing you don't want—get back to your heart and what you truly desire as fast and gently as you can. Or go back to the "make friends with your feelings" chapter and process, share, or express the emotions before continuing on. Anger, fear, or uncertainty may be here, and you get to make friends with these emotions and feelings too, rather than push them away.

Remember to be compassionate when you fall back into the fear or the loop de loop. The mental fear we self-project is vastly different when compared to what it means to love yourself enough to be there when the emotion is felt and expressed out of that beautiful body of yours. If you take a detour into fear or get back on the carousel, simply pause and breathe love into it.

Ask your inner guide and heart, "What do I need right now? What does my body need right now? And what would LOVE do? How would it do it?"

Be with the fear. Sit with it, embrace it gently, and forgive the part of you that believes in fear and love it hard. If this feels difficult, love it hard too. This is where our feelings are our friends, not the enemy. We can love all our feelings and choose which ones we want to lean into most as our superpower. The truth is that the last thing we need is more fear because we have so much living here already. We want to feel as safe, loved, accepted, and connected as can be through every part of the unfolding journey.

Remember when I saw the new osteopath for the first time and the first thing he asked me was "What's your story?" Well, here, and in this moment, we get to create a new one, with our heart. With that feeling of LOVE that is so unconditional that it lights us up and heals us, thought by thought, big feeling by big feeling, neuron by neuron, cell by cell.

One organ and new story at a time—starting with our heart, the most powerful organ of all.

There is scientific evidence as to why this is possible; however, I think we sometimes learn better by experiencing it ourselves—by hearing the stories of what's possible from others and coming to our own discovery and understanding of why they worked. Had I not felt it, I don't know if I would believe it. We must take the belief and really put it into action, again and again, until our new story becomes our new reality.

During that week at the program when I was starting to rewire my thoughts, a.k.a. my brain, with intention, I got the chance to share a story, one that made me happiest and brought me to the biggest feelings of love. Visualizations were a practice I got to learn, and I am going to tell you some more stories! (Wait, this whole book is basically all mini stories; thus, we will keep going.)

Ready to snuggle up for some more story time, a.k.a. visualization time?

Story time is similar to the concept of visualizations or living fully in a moment (remembering it, retelling it, creating it in a way it has not happened yet, and getting to choose a new ending).

It's like when you're a child and someone reads you a story.

You feel the excitement, you get emotional based on the character and what happens, and you're trying to guess what the characters might do. Except here you get to CHOOSE, and you get to make yourself the main character.

When you listen to someone tell a story, you follow the story with your full heart. You feel as the character may feel and you feel some sense of possibility and hope or learning message based on whatever the character shared. We are going to do this together, but you get to visualize and create your own new stories. And embrace each new moment.

My first taste of visualizing was remembering and sharing a past moment. One of those moments was when I was so completely in love with the present that I got out of my head and straight into my heart—straight into the feeling of pure unconditional love. This was a memory from when I was around eighteen years old, and it was about babies. I LOVE babies. Since I was a little kid, I have been like the baby whisperer. If there's a baby around, you know I'd be there, next in line, just waiting to hold that sweet little bundle of pure love. I'm fully in my heart when I am with babies. They mirror pure unconditional love, and I share that feeling too.

I am guessing you're seeing where this is going. This was my chance to share a story that would get me to an elevated emotion, to this BIG LOVE FEELING, and boy, did it ever!

This story is an example of a visualization: vision + feeling = new story/ reality. It's like the idea of smell-o-vision, like having a picture in your mind with a smell alongside it, but in this case, it's a feeling. Please note, however, that you may bring other senses into it like smell, taste, touch, sound, or anything you want! It's your story, your visualization.

So, here is my "story" explained and shared in vivid detail with all the imagery, senses, and FEELINGS included. After all, it does make for a better story, right?!

I remember this day as if it were yesterday. As I stood there in front of the group, ready to share my visualization, I kept forgetting what I was meant to say next, but I was guided so gently and lovingly that in those moments, I felt supported. I felt deeply held and safe to be imperfect and simply do my best. This is the feeling I had always wanted, and it seemed that this was the feeling I went to in that first visualization. I had gone back to an important moment in my life when I met the little girl who holds the most special place in my heart. I went back to the day I first met her.

It was October, and I was visiting home from university, standing at the door of the house of one of my former high school teachers who had always been my mentor, biggest cheerleader, and supporter. We had always had a special bond, and she had become such an important part of my life. She, too, allowed me to feel safe enough to feel all my feelings and feel good enough as I was. I was excited to see her that day, and as I stood knocking at the door with anticipation, there was nothing I could ever want more than to be there right then. I remember her husband answering the door. I was excited to finally meet him after all the years of hearing about her wonderful partner. More than anything, I was excited to meet her brand-new baby girl who was only about two weeks old.

I remember standing in the basement, noticing how the room was decorated, seeing and feeling the baby blanket and smelling that sweet new baby smell. Looking into her big, beautiful blue eyes for the first time, I just knew how much we would learn and grow together from this moment on. I felt a deep sense of unconditional love like I never had before as I sang to her, gently rocking her back and forth. I was so happy and so grateful in this moment. I loved being there and that present moment was everything. She did not have to do anything or be anything to earn it. She was worthy of this love as she was, and as she would always be.

As I stood there in the room, speaking this memory in the present moment, it was as if my whole brain and body believed I was back in that moment right then. I felt my heart expand, I began to cry, and the tears kept coming as I felt full-body love. I was feeling exactly how I felt then, simply by going there in my mind and feeling this emotion in my heart.

What happened in that moment was beyond anything that words can ever do justice. The feelings I experienced then are indescribable, yet I will do my best to describe them here. It was as if this feeling of unconditional love flooded every inch of my body, every cell, every organ, every part of my being. Every single part of my body that needed love felt it in that moment. I knew right then that something big and life changing had just happened. I didn't really understand it, but what I knew was that this feeling of unconditional love was more powerful than anything I had ever felt in the world.

I knew that if I could keep coming back to this feeling, I could use it to heal every part of me that was sick. And truth be told, I could see how every part of me that felt the most unworthy of love had manifested into illness in my own body. I realized that instead of hating my body for what it couldn't or wasn't doing for me, I could love it for how hard it works FOR me and all it is, does, and communicates with me on a daily basis.

I also realized that each part of my body that wanted so badly to heal simply needed more of this unconditional love in order to work again. *Why hadn't I thought of healing in THIS way before? Just like the baby who I could so easily love in all conditions, could I love myself, my body, like this?*

When I could slow down enough to give this to myself, I had a feeling that this was the place where everything would change, and this was when my motto did too. My motto and way of being changed from "fake it until you make it" to "**feel it until you experience it.**"

When I could stop pretending that I was okay when I wasn't and simply start loving every part of me that felt this way, I would be able to get my life back. Or better yet, I would be able to live a new one, one that better served me and came from a place of love and acceptance rather than the fear of not being enough, of not being perfect. I could choose to live a life where I could love every single part of me, without needing to try to fix me or be someone or something in order to be good enough, and allow myself to simply be and love myself unconditionally, perfectly imperfect, exactly as I am.

See, that's what love does. It loves no matter what—whether or not something is working. Just as I looked at the sweet baby girl in that way, feeling unconditional love in my heart and every part of me, it was time for me to start looking at myself that way.

Holding her and feeling unconditional love taught me that more than anything, the whole point of my accident was to learn how to hold myself and see myself with that same unconditional love. It was also time to feel held, loved, and wholeheartedly accepted, and to receive love.

Now, my body was asking for more love, and it was up to me to give it and to receive it too. And this is where I have the power to heal from within, with my heart, with my dreams, and with the knowingness that

I am held and that I'm already whole, worthy, and complete, regardless of what my body is telling me.

My heart knows, and my heart is here to remind every other part when it forgets.

After remembering that experience, I had a dream. It was powerful and really showed me what any healing or remembering journey is all about. In the dream, there were two versions of me. I was there in the present holding four-year-old me, rocking me back and forth like I had with the baby and telling myself that everything was going to be okay. I was looking at myself with the same unconditional love I had felt while looking in her eyes. She was my mirror; she was allowing me to see all the love within me that I saw in her, helping me to be who I am. When I could love myself through the mud that only got bigger after having a brain injury, I could love myself through anything.

When what I thought was my one thing—being smart and achieving—was taken away, yet I could still love myself, I was more empowered than I have ever been. If I could learn to love myself without all the things that I believed made me worthy and good enough, I would always be good enough.

What was more powerful than all, however, was that this "medicine" camc from within. **This medicine is love—it's my heart, it's my feelings, and I am FULL OF FEELINGS. And so are you!**

Here are a few more examples to get your feelings flowing and your can-do mentality ignited. Remember, you CAN guide yourself off that carousel and into the feelings of love, hope, faith, and positivity too. You can also let others help you in the moments it feels hard and you still need a bit of holding.

These are two examples of visualizations or "stories" that you can create. Remember, they may be a stretch from where you are today or what you feel is possible. It's like creating or writing a script or story for an experience you want to have. **You get to create it so get into your imagination, have fun creating a life you want to live, and let your senses guide you.**

I use the present tense so the brain and body get the message that this dream is *actually* happening NOW. This is how we create the possibilities that are to come while letting our body get the healing medicine in this moment.

EXAMPLE 1: THE WEDDING VISUALIZATION

I am SO excited! It is my best friend's wedding day. I am wearing a pretty blue dress. It's soft and flowy and I feel so FREE in it. I am playing one of my favorite songs as we are getting ready. I am twirling around as I am dancing, and my man, whom I love dearly, comes and joins me. I love how much fun we always have together and that he dances with me even when I am at my silliest!

He is my date to the wedding, and we are on our way there. It's as if there is nothing but love songs playing in our car. "Marry You" by Bruno Mars is followed by Ben E. King's "Stand By Me." I feel the love and know it is going to be the most magical day.

Soon enough, we are at the wedding, watching my best friend walk down the aisle. And I feel with all my body this LOVE and excitement for her and her husband (to be), and the collective feeling of love in the room. There are twinkly lights. She is beaming with excitement, and we are all beaming as we watch her lovingly walk (or more like glide) down the aisle. In this moment, though, I look at her groom. His face says it all. There are tears of love streaming down his face and he has the biggest smile I have ever seen. It's pure love, baby!

I take this feeling and let it rise in my body, from my toes to the neurons in my brain to my limbic system, then I do it all again! I can feel it in every cell, every organ, every part wanting a little extra love today, and I know this is the best medicine there is, and it came from my heart and my very vivid imagination. What else could we possibly need?!

EXAMPLE 2: PARENT PLEASURE, PLAY, AND PRESENCE

I am a mama, and I absolutely adore my life. I feel filled with love every day, and I get to do what I love. I have learned how to calm the storm of my mind and find the play and love in my heart when I need it most.

There's this knowingness that I can lean on love when I need it. That when I find this in my own being, my children feel it too. I reflect on how as I have learned to BE LOVE, I can beam love and be present when they are feeling emotions and having a hard moment. And it started with me.

I stopped giving all of me to those around me and instead started with filling my love cup, my heart, first. I didn't do it all at once. I started with compassion. I started with letting my friends and my helpers hold me. I started finding "me time" daily until my time grew. I learned to PLAY again and discover WHAT I LOVE. And I create art again and write in my journal because it reminds me of the love that I am/that we all are and how good it feels to make time to connect solely with me, my heart, and my feelings.

Every day, I make the "not so fun or loving" moments more loving by coming back to my heart, turning up the FUN, and reminding myself that I always have a choice. It's one of those days when I stopped cleaning the house and paused. I breathed in my overwhelm, breathed out, then got back to my heart. My heart reminded me that I needed to play, to connect with myself and my kids. So, we all paused, we all connected, and this time with our hearts leading us. Our hearts wanted to have a dance party.

So, here I am, my heart fuller and more connected than ever, surrounded by a messy playroom. Dancing it out. Our favorite songs are playing, and each of us takes a turn picking the next one. We are making up the silliest dance moves, and all I feel is love and fun. I remind myself that this is healing! **My heart has healed my brain, my body, and I am love**. We are all love, and we're feeling so very loved. Anything is possible, and sometimes the miracle is pausing and dancing with the people I love most. They are my medicine. I am my medicine. And my joy is a priority. I can live the life I want and feel good being a mom!

Now, for the science-loving folks who want the tangible why/the proof:

I was at a speaking engagement where I was sharing my journey. Before presenting, I shared with someone that "love healed me," and I was asked to take that slide out of the PowerPoint. It felt icky to be asked to take it out, mostly because I knew in my heart and in my gut that it was my truth.

But the fear was that it was too "new agey." At the time, I didn't even know what that meant. Well, it turns out I am NOW as "woo-woo" and as "new agey" as you can get. But there was a time that I wasn't even a "woo" because I cared about the rules and about how others viewed me and about doing things the "right" way rather than doing them the way that felt right for me. True for me. This is my truth. This is what helped to heal me, to bring me back to my essence.

And here's the science behind the WHY:

Oxytocin, baby! Oxytocin is often called the "love drug." I remember reading about it around the time I learned about this new way of healing. Oxytocin—a neurotransmitter—is released in the pituitary gland when people cuddle, snuggle, or are physically intimate.

When we are sick and isolated, we can sometimes be severely lacking in the "love drug," and oxytocin can be so helpful in healing ourselves. We may not be able to be around people at this stage in our recovery, but mirror neurons or visualizing doing activities that would secrete oxytocin can actually help our brains produce it. Thus, my visualizations of the wedding and of holding the baby (and whatever visualizations you choose for yourself) can increase the brain's production of oxytocin.

In Bernie Siegel's book *Love, Medicine and Miracles*, he writes, "I am convinced that unconditional love is the most powerful stimulant of the immune system. The truth is: love heals. Even though love is hard to study scientifically, medical research is beginning to confirm its effects. At the Menninger Foundation in Topeka, Kansas, people who are in love, in the romantic sense, have been found to have reduced levels of lactic acid in their blood, making them less tired, and higher levels of endorphins, making them euphoric and less subject to pain. Their white blood cells also responded better when faced with infections, and thus got fewer colds. In 1982, Harvard psychologists David McClelland

and Carol Kirshnit found that even movies about love increase levels
of immunoglobulin-A in saliva, the first line of defense against colds
and viral diseases."

But what Siegel also reminds his readers of is that although love can
heal and increase these healthful things, "the idea is to love because it
feels good, not because it will [heal us]. Love is the end itself, not the
means. Love makes life worth living. It also increases the likelihood of
physical healing, but that is the bonus, the icing on the cake."

And when we consciously choose to love and lean into our heart
when our brain wants to go wild with panic and fear, we release these
neurotransmitters and oxytocin by feeling love, which then links the
production of this "love drug."

Babies are often associated with oxytocin. When a mother is holding
or feeding her baby, snuggling the baby close to her heart, she is feeling love and releasing a lot of oxytocin. Sex is also another activity that
produces this "love drug" in our brains. But if you're not having any, no
worries! Sex was definitely not something I could even bring myself to
think about doing at the time. The mere thought of it would have done
the opposite of secreting oxytocin! If this thought brings you love, connection, and oxytocin, you can visualize it too. Or visualize whatever
activities or experiences you desire, as it will allow the neurotransmitters
to release the "feel good" hormones that will support your body in its
healing and make life worth living.

One of the things I learned is that oxytocin is a neurotransmitter, and
depending on our feelings and thoughts, our brain can elicit a number of
neurotransmitters that tend to be linked to our fight-or-flight response.

So, when we get into our heart, we change the neurotransmitters that are secreted, which changes the pathways and our "expected" response in the future. For example, when we were in the loop before and in a constant stress state, our go-to neurotransmitters were cortisol, adrenaline, and norepinephrine, the main three stress hormones. Whereas when we get to that lovey-dovey state with elevated emotions, we tend to shift into secreting neurotransmitters like dopamine, oxytocin, serotonin, and endorphins. These are our happy hormones!

And last, the heart has the most powerful electromagnetic field, and something known as "heart-brain coherence" can be a big healer by tapping into the heart to balance the brain. According to the HeartMath Institute, "The heart is the most powerful source of electromagnetic energy in the human body, producing the largest rhythmic electromagnetic field of any of the body's organs. The heart's electrical field is about 60 times greater in amplitude than the electrical activity generated by the brain. This field, measured in the form of an electrocardiogram (ECG), can be detected anywhere on the surface of the body. Furthermore, the magnetic field produced by the heart is more than 100 times greater in strength than the field generated by the brain and can be detected up to 3 feet away from the body, in all directions." This might mean nothing to you. Perhaps you're even wondering what the heck it even means, which is completely okay. I would have questioned it too.

Let this new awareness sink into the body. All it needs to understand is that feeling elevated feelings like appreciation and love and having awareness of when the heart is coherent and congruent with these emotions will support the brain to get there too. Sometimes sickness creates a lot of what is called "incoherence" in both the heart and brain, which constant states of stress can induce.

This is why breathing into our heart and finding new ways to tap into the love and gratitude feelings can shift the heart into a state of coherence, which will further support the brain to match this greater frequency. The HeartMath Institute also states that "numerous studies have since shown that heart coherence is an optimal physiological state associated with increased cognitive function, self-regulatory capacity, emotional stability and resilience."

All these are things, which, after a brain injury and trauma, can become difficult to manage and navigate. Thus, it would be wise to shift our focus from worrying about these capacities with our head and let our brain get along with the wisdom the heart already knows. Our body is innately wise and aware of what it needs to rest, relax, recover, heal, and thrive. It's time to lean into that more, breathe into it, and allow ourselves to feel our way to heal what needs to be healed. When we can do that, we can more easily let our feeling superpowers enhance our state and move into coherence.

NOW ON TO YOUR FEELING SUPERPOWER:

The reason I shared my superpower and story is because for me, LOVE was my go-to emotion during my healing. And that may be personal for me. Some other feeling may be your superpower. Here is something that might help you get in touch with YOU and your go-to feeling, the one that feels like the biggest and most powerful medicine for your journey. Yours may be different from mine because you are you, and that is the most beautiful thing of all.

Take a peek at the words below and feel into your heart. Which ones are easy to get to, to sustain, and to feel over and over again? Highlight or circle the ones that most resonate:

Love

Compassion

Joy

Play

Gratitude

Acceptance

Peace

Freedom

Kindness

Being nurtured or cared for

Worthiness

Calmness

Limitless

Think of some of your favorite moments that have already occurred or moments you want to have. What is the predominant feeling behind them? How do you feel in those moments?

This exercise will help you find your own feeling superpower! Come back to it often. Feel it fully.

Let's use our superpowers!

TAKEAWAY & P L A Y

To put it into action. Claim your feelings below.

My superpower feeling is: _____

Now it's time to have some fun. In your journal, write out your feeling-visions in the present tense (as if they are happening now).

- It's time to create your new story, and most importantly, feel the feelings in those moments. And then let those feelings expand and grow.
- How can it get even better?
- How can you infuse more love and (insert your feeling here) than this?

To help you get into it, here is a meditation to guide you through the process: https://www.mindbodysoulmiracles.com/eat-play-love

Listen to it and feel the feeling, the vision, then write out what you experienced, so when you need to be reminded to come back to the heart and the feeling in the loop de loop moments, you can. Then breathe into your heart, grab your journal, read it over, and do it again!

Chapter 11

FROM FIGHT OR FLIGHT TO STAY AND PLAY

To play with life as it plays with you.

-Unknown

The things we seek are seeking us too. And one day while I was online, an ad popped up that reminded me. It was a huge aha moment that pieced together my own philosophy of healing for me. **To stay and play.**

Remember how in the chapter about childhood, I shared that my coping mechanism was to "run or hide" or shut down and just cry? What if instead, I stayed . . . and played?

"From fight or flight to stay and play" is what I heard that day from meditation teacher and author Emily Fletcher. This was around the time I had finally discovered the purpose and re-integration of play as something incredibly important, in fact 100 percent vital, to our ability to not just survive but thrive. And to move beyond those patterns that have been keeping us stuck.

Bear with me, my skeptics, who think play is not for grown-ups or that there is no time for it. I was you, and you, likely, are like me in that play is exactly what you need more than anything. You don't need one more medical practitioner telling you what supplement to take, what protocol to try, or what next specialist to see. You need something for you. You need something that will give you a reason to keep going, to get up in the morning if you still aren't feeling quite like you yet. You need the thing that reminds you of who YOU are. The thing that lights you up. The thing that brings meaning to your world, your heart, your soul, your whole being. The thing that helps you remember you are already whole, even in those moments when you still feel a bit broken or in need of fixing.

The epigraph at the beginning of this chapter pretty well sums up how life is meant to be lived, and sometimes we miss the mark completely because, much like the child who cared about achieving the good grades, we forgot to play as hard as we worked. I finally get what that quote means: Life isn't meant to be so hard. It isn't about striving for perfection or getting it right or always doing or learning without having the time to just be.

It's like the Game of Life—filled with choices, twists, turns, and new chapters, and we get to choose! We get to make the next move, something that can be scary, but what if we get to have FUN with this part? What if life really is much like a game?

Think about that for a second. What if life is a game that is meant to be played, all in—the whole thing—having fun, playing, enjoying each moment, immersing ourselves in growth, and loving ourselves every step of the way? Maybe it really is about taking ourselves less seriously and honoring the silliness and humanness in moments when laughter or fun is truly the best medicine. Nobody ever discovered inner peace by stressing their way through each day! Believe that laughter is yours for the taking, and play is yours for the making!

You may be new to this perspective, much like I was, and you may even think, *What does she mean by PLAY?*

I am going to fill you in and hold you in this new way because you may be resisting play, or you may not be making it an important, crucial, prioritized part of your day. I know that up until this point, I hadn't listed play as one of the priorities in my agenda. It wasn't important and was often left until/if I had time remaining after getting through the things I needed to do. Yet if I had taken the time to be, to play, to reconnect with me, the things that needed doing would have been a bit easier and more enjoyable for me.

But we aren't there right now. We are still covered in sludge, trekking through our mud or feeling very triggered through this healing process. There may still be that feeling that despite "all the things" we are doing to heal, they still don't feel like ENOUGH! (And you may be realizing you're not having much FUN.) Despite this, you do feel more empowered now that you have lots of new tools to help and finally a greater sense of HOPE for maybe the first time ever. We finally have most of the ingredients in our new "funner" recipe for healing ready to go.

Did you have an Easy-Bake Oven as a kid? We're ready to put the ingredients together so we can bake that teeny tiny cake and finally have some FUN while doing it. We're taking off the pressure to do it the "right" way; instead, we're going to play house. Put on your favorite song and sing along while we let that little cake bake as long as it needs to.

I always felt that invisible but ever-present pressure to be "doing," especially since doing anything had taken me so much longer since my diagnosis. It made me realize that maybe the perfectionist in me had always been that way. Maybe my incessant need to "get it right" made it that much harder to a) play, and b) get things done in a timely manner. If I had let go of "perfect," maybe I would have gotten things done a little quicker or just not cared quite so much about every single thing the way I did.

But that's how I'd functioned since I was a child. Everything had to be just right. And once I got into first or second grade, play wasn't as important because all that pressure to learn, to achieve, to get things right zapped so much of the fun out of life.

Why do we lose play? When did it stop being important to us?

Sometimes life has a way of bringing us back to the basics and reminding us about what truly matters. At least, this journey did that for me. It brought me back to playing. Since all I used to do was actually DO, until I was unable to anymore, **play became the prescription I needed most**.

When we forget to make play a priority and focus too hard on the doing, the fixing of the problem, and the finding of an answer, we get stuck in that way of being for far too long.

It's like the saying, "a watched pot never boils." I remember hearing this phrase a lot as a kid. I would be reminded of it while sitting at the window waiting for someone to come over or while anticipating something I was really excited about (think Christmas morning or your birthday!). I have a vivid memory of waiting impatiently for my Chuck E. Cheese birthday party. We often count sleeps before the big day arrives ("just two more sleeps until . . ."), but when it comes to matters of our health, we're pretty much pulling our hair and thinking, *Seriously, how many more sleeps, gosh darn it?!*

My internal monologue used to be *Are we there yet? Are we there yet?*

And when it comes to our health, our internal monologue inevitably turns to *Why am I not better yet? When will I finally feel better? I can't do this anymore.*

My answer now to living is to start playing again. To understand the "why," I will share a little more.

Just like looking out the window made it feel like it took even longer for the person or big day to arrive, and just like waiting for that pot to boil, we've been waiting impatiently for the healing to begin.

The pot needs to go through the necessary steps to boil. It needs to heat up first, and that takes time. Inevitably, when we stop watching the pot with the expectation for it to heat up and boil right away, it eventually does in its own timing. We need to let go and trust that it will do what it's meant to do.

Our healing journey is similar, especially if we've been constantly watching our symptoms and bodies (like that pot). When we do the symptom managing and checking and the googling about our labels and diagnoses, when we focus on fixing by trying one protocol followed by the next, we place immense pressure on the outcome we desire. Our constant doing makes the situation more stressful, as does our constant worrying if this next action or treatment or medication will finally be the one to make all the symptoms go away. It can be really frustrating, disempowering, and disheartening! It isn't so easy to wait when it is something you really and truly want.

And I know you. You are just like me. I so badly wanted to LIVE again and have my life back, but it turns out that the things I was doing to get it back were actually stopping me from being able to live. To enjoy the present moment. And part of living is playing. When we play, we forget about the things we need or want because we are wholeheartedly present in the now. And the here and now is pretty wonderful indeed. When we are completely engaged in things that bring us the most joy, the most love, the most connection, and the most PLAY (the most yay!), we are living!

What experiences, activities, or games help you to feel this way?

When was the last time you PLAYED?

When was the last time you did something just for the FUN of it?

When was the last time you did something without an outcome, without a focus, without an agenda? Just because!

Play time is when we finally stop looking at the pot! We consciously choose to allow what we want to happen by taking our focus and pressure off our bodies while doing what we love most. Some of you may still be in the imagining phase of feeling into the possibilities and remembering games or ways we like to play. That's completely okay. In time, this will help you try those things again because your elevated state will allow your body to feel as if it's possible. This is enough to eventually get back into doing those things. Remember that playing is *being*. It's also *daydreaming* and *imagining*. Don't let anyone tell you otherwise.

The world often belongs to the dreamers, the visionaries, and the hopelessly optimistic humans who are filled with so much love! They are the changemakers, the movers and shakers, the creatives, the misfits, and the so-called weirdos! So, sitting cozy in bed and daydreaming about the experiences you have had or wish to have, or the imaginary trips you desire, or the partner you want, or your future babies or fur babies counts!

Playing and daydreaming can take the pressure off YOU and your healing and simply let the BODY "do its THANG."

By "do its thang," I mean decrease symptoms and heal. The nervous system is in control here. A lot of our "safety" has come from controlling, and we are scared that if we don't control, we won't get better. Our desire to constantly be the one in control of how we heal is the very thing that is in the way of us actually getting better.

When we control, we hold, we breathe less, and we stress more. We remain stuck in fight or flight, constantly keeping us in sympathetic mode.

The nervous system is made up of two functions: our sympathetic nervous system and the parasympathetic nervous system. When the sympathetic nervous system is switched on, we are in fight-or-flight mode. And some of us may be sensitive to hitting the "on" button that activates our sympathetic nervous system.

However, when we turn on the parasympathetic nervous system, we enter a rest, digest, repair, and regenerate state where healing happens naturally! Our bodies are amazing and can self-heal when we enter this state. So, let's let the fun begin!

Something to gently and kindly remind your mind of when it wants to control, fix, do, and focus is that it's making it difficult for your body to get into a healing state.

Chances are you were wired as a child to be easily triggered into stress mode, expecting something bad to happen. Thus, constantly having your sympathetic nervous system activated could be your resting state (or your easily "switched on" state). It makes sense that the trauma loop is easily activated after a childhood where trauma (big or little) was present and then a bigger trauma, illness, injury, or accident happened.

The brain can change, and it can rewire and change through play. We can easily enter our parasympathetic nervous system. Dr. Karyn B. Purvis states that "scientists have discovered that it takes approximately 400 repetitions to create a new synapse in the brain, unless it is done in play, in which case, it only takes 10 to 20 repetitions."

The parasympathetic nervous system is where the magic happens, but for some people, that state can feel unfamiliar. This is often what happens when children grow up with low-level or high-level anxiety and stress, or they are super sensitive (which sometimes means little things feel bigger in their body). Stress is their baseline, and they may have gotten used to *doing* more than *being*, to *stressing* more than *playing*, and to *controlling* a lot more than trusting or knowing they are *safe*. This is especially true for highly sensitive people, often referred to as empaths. When we don't feel safe, we want to run and hide, or we enter that freeze state where nothing really happens. **Here is where we flip the switch, from sympathetic to parasympathetic, from fight or flight to stay and play!**

This gets to be our new way and our new homeostasis, our baseline, which makes life about thriving and playing rather than surviving.

Sometimes coming home to yourself also means coming back to your PLAY.

Getting into the parasympathetic nervous system allows the healing to happen naturally without us doing anything at all. When we hit the switch and get into the parasympathetic state, our bodies know exactly what to do and how to do it without us controlling anything. This is **magical** to me, and what I learned was that it isn't always easy to control or "not think" of the thing you want to happen when it's something as important as your health. And when your body/brain has been so used to doing and living in a constant state of expected stress, it can mean shifting a lot to try a completely new way, which involves a lot of play.

Ultimately, what did get me out of my head and into my heart, and most importantly, what helped me stay there, focused in each present moment, was PLAY! This was the way I needed to heal when I was still overdoing it all, when I was trying to fix everything, when I was focusing on the rules and the protocols and what other practitioners believed was best for my body and healing.

I was in need of more play, more joy, more love, and more connection.

I once heard trauma defined as a loss of connection. And there is nothing that connects us more to others or ourselves than pure unstructured play without any expectations; we are connected simply with the idea of bonding, of sharing, of creating. Play is how we integrate!

Play takes the pressure off. Play takes the focus off the "when will this happen" and brings us deeply into the here and now.

When we constantly look at ourselves and our bodies as a problem to be fixed, we add too much pressure. When we are engaged in something we love, our body feels that same love.

We don't need to constantly live in the stressful state of focusing on when something will happen. Let's stay in the here and now, live as if it (our health and happiness) has arrived, and play our way through the day.

Time to get back to the basics and take a trip to "little" you first.

Chances are that your inner child (your little you) knew how to play! We need to tap back into that part of us while remembering the good parts, the happy moments, the FUN!

How did you play as a child? What thing (or things) did you do when it felt like time came to a standstill, especially when you were so immersed in doing these things? My definition of play is doing the thing you love doing so much that when you're doing it, it's as if all time goes away!

One of my favorite games to play when I was little was House (and School, Teacher, Doctor, and all those fun role-playing games). I loved the House Center in kindergarten, and I would ALWAYS play "the mom" to the other children. I also remember having a pet polar bear (so random and also so Canadian!).

It won't come as a surprise to you that I loved playing with dolls. I remember my favorite birthday present as a child was getting a set of triplet baby dolls: two girls and a boy. It was the best gift ever! I would rock them, hold them, snuggle them lovingly, feed them, sing to them, change their diapers, and go for stroller walks. This was how I played! This was love and joy for little me.

I also had many Barbies, Ken dolls, little Kelly and Tommy toddler dolls, and about five Barbie babies (also a triplet set in there). I remember always playing out the same story: Barbie and Ken meet, date, and fall madly in love. I would then have them act out a very creative wedding (with my VHS movies lined up to be the aisle and with our keyboard playing the organ anthem as Barbie glided down the aisle in her very beautiful white dress and veil). Ken would kiss the bride and Barbie would get pregnant and have lots and lots of babies. It's pretty obvious what lights me up!

I also loved playing Jenga with my entire family (cousins, aunts, uncles, and grandparents included). In our family, we often played it on birthdays when we were all together. When we made the tower fall, we would write our name on the block that made it fall. It was fun to see our names over the years and to remember the memories we shared.

As I grew a bit older, I eventually moved on to a computer-based CD-ROM game, *The Sims*. It required the same imagination in creating my own life (like Barbies did), but it had more things to consider and more creating and playing options—and the ability to create the people in each family and play out their life. I think *The Sims* is how I played, visualized, and daydreamed. And it's safe to say that I loved that I could create a family and allow them to have children, watch the children grow and learn, get jobs, and support the social interactions of the people who were playing with me.

I also loved playing the Game of Life with friends because it showed our personalities, what mattered to us, and how we had a choice in each stage of our lives: Do I want to go to university or start a career? Do I want to have children? What kind of home do I want to live in? Playing this game showed me how life could be full of possibilities and choices.

Let's take what we learned from our favorite games and get back into this way of life! Let's take that same play and bring it into your present—into your adulthood and into your current circumstance—to allow you to heal.

Play is what helped me to heal. And I want to share the conclusion I came to as a result. I feel that part of getting sick was about allowing me to give myself full permission to play. I needed this prescription to prioritize play. Life could truly be more joyful, more playful, and more focused on the now and less centered on outcomes and potential things that could go wrong in the future.

I decided to use a few pointers from the children in my life, then help these bring me back to that state.

Enter the children: a.k.a. our biggest teachers (and definitely mine!). The ones who have fun no matter what they do, who can create something from nothing, and who have endless creative ideas and ways to take the simple tasks in life and turn them into a game.

I spent a few months babysitting and playing. We played our favorite songs, had endless dance parties, and went on long nature walks. We played I spy, made forts in the living room, colored, played with play-dough, did arts and crafts, and dressed up.

Baking was also a fun way for us to play. We made chocolate chip cookies and banana bread, as well as totally gross (but safe) concoctions to see who would eat it (think *Fear Factor*).

We built snowmen and played Capture the Flag and Hide-and-Seek. We watched our favorite movies while snuggled up all together on the couch. We watched *The Wiggles*, and we sang and laughed and danced alongside them. We stayed and PLAYED.

I got better by doing joyful things in life while increasing my ability to do tasks I once wasn't able to. The joy allowed my body to do its thang and get what it needed.

Sometimes my way of playing would be more adult-like too, like reading (often a mixture of neuroplasticity/healing-focused books, fun fiction, and ones on spirituality and personal growth). I also did yoga, walked, meditated, visualized, caught up with a friend over tea, and played with babies and puppies (because I can't stress the health benefits of this more: hello, oxytocin!).

Life is about the little things, and children are the reminders we need for how to approach the hard things in life in a new, playful, easy, creative, and imaginative way! When we enter this playful and creative state, we let go of our limitations!

When we focus on that thing we are afraid might not happen for us, it's hard to enter our creative state. **It's time to tap into FUN and let PLAY guide our way forward!**

I remember being asked what my favorite movie was while I was in a fight-or-flight pressure state, and I couldn't answer the question. But once I got back into my relaxed state by playing, the answer came to me. Sometimes that's how play helps us heal, by helping us get back into our homeostasis and into a state where we *can receive*. Things seem clearer when we're relaxed and happy.

I have such happy memories of my sister and me watching my favorite movie, *The Sound of Music*, at my grandmother's apartment. There is a wonderful scene that really captures the essence of neuroplasticity. It's the first time that Maria bonds with the children. They're scared because there's a storm outside, so they all come into her room for some comfort. Maria sings about what she does when she is feeling scared. I'm sure you know and love it too: "My Favorite Things." By focusing on what makes her happy, she's able to cope with her fear, and that is how neuroplasticity works: it creates a new loop in the brain by replacing triggering feelings with positive ones.

And that is what play does. When we are triggered, when the fear arises, we need to pause, step back, and PLAY. We can act, imagine, visualize, talk, or even SING about our favorite things to help us create a new loop and a new reality. We can also turn it into a game, like the von Trapp family did, by sharing our worries with someone we trust who can comfort us so the fear doesn't seem as big and scary anymore. But we get to do it in a FUN way that stresses the joy, the love, the connection, and the play rather than staying focused or worried on the fears.

TAKEAWAY & PLAY

It's time to start being in your power by playing.

It's time to play one of my favorite games: the "What Makes Me Happy" game. I made up the game and the name, but you can call it whatever you like. Here's how this game works:

Play with one person (or more). One person shares something first.

Person 1: (Names something that makes them happy.) "Going to the beach when it's really hot out and making a sand castle!"
Person 2: (Can comment on it or simply share their happy thing.) "Ooh, I love the beach too! My favorite thing to do is to have an ice cream cone with the people I love when it gets warm out. I love chocolate chip cookie dough ice cream!"
Person 1: "Mmm, my fave is mint chocolate chip. Something else that makes me happy is having a bonfire where we sing and my friends bring their guitars and we get to dance and snuggle under blankets."

You get the point. You play as long as you want and sometimes as long as it takes to raise the state you are in and get back into play . . . until you feel more like you again!

TAKEAWAY & P L A Y

IT'S JOURNAL TIME:

- How did you love to play as a child?
- What were your top five games to play and what did you love most about them?
- How do you play now? (Remember that there are no wrong answers or ways to play.)
- Try a new "stay and play" challenge. Devote a certain amount of time each day to diving back into your play! For example, choose twenty minutes of "you time" simply to do something playful! Maybe you try this five days per week, or you start small and then increase! (Come up with ways to play on your own and ways to play with the people you love most!) Then let yourself be ALL IN and fully enjoy this time for JOY!

You know best what lights you up, makes your heart sparkle, and helps you tap into the magic! Let yourself be guided to new ways to play and get out of your head and back into the present moment. Remember, that's where your parasympathetic nervous system guides the way and your body can and will do its thang (heal).

TAKEAWAY & P L A Y

Play can look different for everyone, and your play may simply be starting where you are, continuing to visualize, daydream, and imagine until you feel (mostly) ready to try it and get back out there. Then start doing something every day to tap back into your playful and creative side. Notice when you find yourself feeling stressed or stuck in your Ps (perfectionism, performing, people-pleasing, or another protective pattern) again. Those are the moments to pause, to find your fun, to play, and to be guided to the new way and the new YOU.

And if you have any questions or feel stuck, don't forget to pray, to ask for help, or to connect with a trusted friend, mentor, or coach. I am here for you and with you and know that this is where the breakthroughs REALLY happen.

Chapter 12

MOVING THROUGH THE FEARS WITH LOVE AND ACCEPTANCE

Nothing is impossible, the word itself says I'm possible.

–Audrey Hepburn

Here is where we take what we've learned and put it into action. Like, actually go do the darn thing! And here is also where it got tricky for me. So, I'm going to keep it real, share with you the wins, the "where it went well" moments, and the flops, where I completely flopped on my face, revisited the fear loop, or took too much of a leap when a baby step was needed.

I share it all with you so you can learn from my mistakes while being gentle, courageous, and compassionate with yourself and with me for feeling safe to laugh at them now, to feel at peace with, and finally, to share them with you. Know that you won't get it right or perfect every single time, and that's kind of the point.

I want to share with you what worked and what didn't work so you can take it all in and let it inform your personal journey, while having fun with it. Fun is our flashlight here.

When we feel the fear, the point isn't to make it go away, it's to use the tools we have and find a way through. I'm going to break that down for you.

But first, I really loved this quote and felt it may resonate with what we are about to do. This is a quote by Stephen Levine:

"To heal is to touch with love that which was previously touched by fear."

I truly believe I healed in this way (and continue to heal whenever a trigger or learning experience presents itself in my life).

Wherever there was pain, wherever there was hurt, wherever I avoided or was too scared to try or face the potential consequences, there was fear there. Often, when we start with the medical route and focus only on the symptoms and figuring out how to treat them, we start to limit, avoid, and stop. Or we become too scared to engage in some parts of our life, which then makes them eventually too scary to do again. For example, when we are sick and overwhelmed with just functioning and getting through the day, there can be a lot of activities in life that we simply stop doing. This can make it hard to move forward and live the life we really want.

So, with that quote in mind, at absolutely any time, tap into the heart when your fear gets really big. We have already started this practice but now we have more ingredients to integrate with it.

But before we start getting INTO it, I want to share from my heart.

Fear wasn't something I was guided to be with, embrace, or even let "be there" because the mind was in "control" yet again in how I was learning to rewrite my story, rewire my brain, and "get back in the game" . . . of living, working, and relating. But my way is to literally get back in the game by first playing a game or finding your FUN, so you can breathe more, be in your parasympathetic nervous system, and maybe even have a laugh while learning something new from whatever you are engaging in as your "play." Stay with me here.

There is a four-step process I take myself and clients through. My Personalized Private Coaching Program is called "Love and Acceptance Coaching." If you hadn't guessed yet, there is something we are going to do that has to do with simply loving, accepting, and connecting to whatever is here. EVEN FEAR!

I know there are a lot of systems and programs in the world that focus on "mindset" and changing the brain with the brain and focusing on controlling the mind and the mental part of changing the thoughts you have. I'm not saying this is bad, it just doesn't feel as loving or serving for people who have sensitive superpowers. I also feel like it is counterproductive to supporting the "protective patterns" already in place, like perfectionism. Needing to "get your thoughts right and positive" can amp up the perfectionist part, which is all about control instead of compassion and messily taking imperfect action. Or playing while you practice.

The mental game isn't the one I want to teach, per se. Because PLAY is so much easier, more fun, and faster . . . not to mention a little more forgiving and compassionate when we add love, acceptance, and connection to our play.

Because LOVE and our visualizations were the biggest superpower and tool for us already, we will always have that to come back to. This is the thing: you can rewire your brain and rewrite your story using the thought-pattern shift or finding a new way through a challenging moment or new experience by "thinking your way" to create a new loop in your brain. But in my way, we "stay and play" and LOVE and accept our fears while following them up with facing them, intuitively, imperfectly, never quite "fully ready." Doing the dang thing when we are not quite as scared as we used to be because our tools and our pure presence has helped us get there.

Here is where I break it down (no, not break-dancing. But hey! If that's how you like to play, do that first before you get back to the "do-ing" of things again.)

You will be doing things again that you might not have done in a looooong time. This is often the way we create new neural connections or new responses to where we may have some fear or triggers, but sometimes just doing the thing again is what we need in order to know we can.

When we have been sick and are in the process of healing or doing everything to get better, we likely haven't been able to DO all the things that bring us connection, safety in relationships, or the joy we want. We don't have the life we want, one without symptoms, and our fear or anxiety is making it difficult to be fully present or enjoy. Chances are, we have a ton of fear in these areas.

If we have been taught the "mind control and change your thoughts right away" way, this likely makes us more scared—scared to be scared.

So, we are not going to do that here because if you're a full-heart feeler (like I am), this will loop you back in and make it harder to create these new shifts. Instead, we are going to fully open our heart to the fear. We will alchemize it by accepting it, fully wholeheartedly, and then we'll PLAY!

I courageously moved through a lot of fears to heal myself, and I also dove right into the fear at times too. This wasn't wrong or bad, it was part of the learning, but it helped me understand how to honor fear and then greet it. This is where we play in the places we used to fear, avoid, and protect (and maybe even feared rejection).

It takes courage to do this part. It takes willingness to fuck it up, to get it wrong, and to look like an idiot who doesn't always feel confident while facing the fear. But I wouldn't be who and where I am today if I hadn't committed to choosing love (and a bit of bravery) amid the things, experiences, and activities that scared (and scare) me most.

I think this is sometimes something I forget, and this chapter is giving the gift of it all so your journey is easier and you get curious rather than judgmental when you are lacking in the love department. We might want to face these fears with love, yet sometimes the fear rears its head a little more. Let that be okay.

But first, let's look at "fear" for a minute. Because sometimes we can do two things:

Face

Everything

And

Rise (ideal . . . am I right?!)

Or

Fuck

Everything

And

RUN! (Let's be honest . . . we've all been here.)

I share this knowing the fear response can create a lot of running, hiding, the Ps, and many protective measures that are doing their best to make sure we don't hurt, whether that be emotional or physical hurt or health symptoms and challenges worsening.

We have been avoiding. We sometimes hide to stop ourselves from hurting more than we may be already. But we eventually want to face the fears, which is where our greatest shifts happen. This is where we get to do it differently, with new possibility . . . with our "stay and play" way. We have slower reintroductions to things that are scary for us while also building up our courage, connection, and love muscles. We must love and accept even the biggest FEARS as they come up and then break them down into manageable steps to find our new way forward. We need to stay and play, let our parasympathetic nervous system turn on, and then face the fear when the fear feels a little less "OMG let's run!" kind of scary. Because that, my friend, is love, and love rewires the brain and our pain. And that is how we move through the mud.

We RISE while raising our belief in our ability to be present and to experience certain experiences, people, places, or fears again. This is how we rewire our responses so these fears are no longer fears. But this happens progressively—it's a process, and a daily thing. We need to face it with a full heart and with a willingness to "get it wrong," but with a heart willing to accept whatever comes our way and whatever needs to be seen or witnessed to let the new in.

My intention is to help you move through your fears with more ease than I did, using the compassion that lives inside of you (your heart) and without the fear of getting it wrong or being afraid to ask for help yet again. It's okay and safe to be afraid, to share your fears and vulnerabilities here, to try, try, and keep trying, and to let every choice, every win, every aha moment inform your next step.

Don't let the big flops scare you from taking another step in the direction of your dreams or from believing that how you want to feel and the experiences you want to have are possible. They are, I can attest to that. I am living proof of that.

When the fear arises, keep coming back to the heart.

Slow down, place your hand on your heart and BREATHE, build up your courage muscles, and keep going. Use the compassion tools from Chapter 6 and remember that where there is the most fear, we might need a little extra help on our side. Refer to Chapter 5 and pray some more (and ask for help, guidance, or a new way or a new guide along the way). You're going for more here, and it's okay to go back before you go forward. There is no right way. **You are the map**, and the twists, turns, and detours are sometimes the way. There really are no wrong turns, there's simply a recalculation of your next route and its coordinates. You are your own GPS; trust that your body and heart will guide you to exactly what you need, when you need it.

But also, let's remind you of the steps we have talked about while giving you that clear four-step process when FEAR rears its head and you're ready to face it with your full heart!

Step 1) **Name the fear.** (Or the pain, shame, or pattern coming up for you.)

Example: I am scared to go to a social gathering because being around people used to be hard for me or overstimulate me, as I felt anxiety or the emotions of the people in the room.

Step 2) **Love and accept whatever the fear is, exactly as it is.** (Alchemize it by holding space for the fear to simply BE HERE, to express that you are here to simply allow for it and not try to change it . . . yet somehow, by not trying to change it, *acceptance* shifts this fully.) Don't believe me? Try this process out for yourself! Acceptance means you can be okay, even if it never changes.

Share this or hold the space for your fear. If you need to start by simply acknowledging it, go slowly. You can lean into acceptance when you get more comfortable with holding this space for yourself. If it's hard, have someone hold that loving and accepting space for you.

Connect with the fear that is present before moving into new possibilities. You can even say to your fear, "I am willing to see you, and I welcome in a new possibility or way to play through it."

ROLE-PLAY or grab your puppets, stuffed animals, or Barbie dolls to act it out. You are going to have a dialogue with the fear, then move into acceptance while loving it as it is, right here.

This is a play-based healing exercise I use sometimes, and it is inspired by a coaching tool I learned in Elementum Coaching Institute, inspired by Gestalt Therapy, known as the Empty Chair Process. It is a great way to dialogue and love on and accept the fear.

Never done something like this before? Check out an example right here:

(Before you do, grab one object or "character" to be you and another to represent "fear." In my example, I use a Barbie doll to represent "me," and I use a rubber chicken to represent "fear." Let fun guide your way here too! Remember, we don't have to take even our fear so seriously.)

Me/Barbie doll: "Hey, fear, I'm right here. What are you feeling?
Fear/the chicken: (shares)
Me/Barbie doll: "Thanks for telling me how you feel. I can imagine that feels scary and a lot to carry. I love you and can accept you exactly as you are right now. I'm not going anywhere. I'm staying right here. I'm listening. Tell me more. I want to

make sure you feel heard. I love you and accept you, even if you are scared. We don't need to make this wrong; you are safe."

Fear/the chicken: (May need to share something else or may want to simply be witnessed here.)

Me/Barbie doll: "I'm happy to move forward at the pace that you need, one scary thing at a time. How can I help you and love you right here? What do you need from me to feel less afraid?"

Continue this role-play until it feels "complete."

If the fear needs to answer, let "fear" or "the chicken character" speak and you as the "Barbie doll" just listen. Let fear speak. Let fear feel heard. That is enough. That is what acceptance is. Listening without interrupting.

Reflect on what you hear and let it be here, fully. Chances are that changes will happen simply by being present to the fear without needing to "make it go away."

Step 3) **Pause, step away & PLAY!** (Being with the process we learned in Chapter 11 and moving beyond "fight or flight" by playing and staying, even if fear is here. Instead of running or going into "fight or flight," we are choosing to slow down, pause, and play through it. This is where we activate the parasympathetic nervous system before and after facing a fear to soothe the nervous system and remind yourself that "you can.")

Notice that the fear got smaller by "being with it with love and acceptance."

Now, if the fear is still big, leaning on play is the next best step.

Play a game, do a dance, belt out your favorite songs, read a book, or meditate on it. Let yourself be guided to a show or movie that is somehow going to support you to feel safe enough, confident enough, or ready to move forward, even if the fear is still there. The key is to lessen the fear and make it so you feel safe enough to face the thing you're scared of or avoiding. First, remember what you truly want beyond the fear and bring in your "why." Let this why (what will be possible by doing the thing) be even bigger than the amount of fear that may be left.

The why is the whole reason you are ready to move through the fear and form a new association. Often, doing the thing is actually what creates the connection, the confidence, or the courage to remember that your dreams and desires truly are possible and within reach. So be with the process and play your way until you are ready for more. This will lead you to Step 4.

Step 4) **Face your fear.** (Go do the darn thing!)

Now, before you go facing all your fears, here is where I break it down and share it with you to guide you to make informed "one next step at a time" loving choices, one step and fear at a time.

A big reminder before you go facing your fears: We are going to CELEBRATE everything.

Celebration is key.

Can you celebrate just being on the road, just being in the game and moving forward, no matter the pace? Play may be the step that makes the fear less big and more fun, but celebrating your courage can help, even if you mess up and flop right into awkward land (funny story to come).

Every way you go takes you where you're going, and perhaps the point of the journey is also fully loving every step, every detour, every wrong exit, and being in that moment to the fullest. Remember the feeling is where the power lies, as is your ability to be present in it. You don't need to label any feeling as bad or wrong but rather notice and become aware of the places it feels hardest to be present. Let this inform your next step and what you may need to move through it.

Know that your "feeling superpowers" and the four-step process are there for you. You can tap into this when the merry-go-round comes back. Remember that your power also lies in receiving support in the way you need it most. You can allow others to hold you, support you, and celebrate you every step of the way. There's no shame in that. This chapter is where the ACTION steps come in, where we actually get back on the road—one where the brain is rewired around the biggest fears, one trip and gas station stop at a time. Don't forget that those pauses are equally as important in moving you forward. This is a journey, remember? You cannot stop believing!

But if you do, remember that it's just fear. Remember that fear is pretty normal, especially when we are disempowered by some sort of diagnosis, when someone puts a label on us or confirms all the illnesses we have. That is when we often start living in this place of fear. Without ever realizing when or how it happens, we feel afraid of even the simplest things because to us, they feel dangerous. They feel like triggers that keep us sick. We limit our activities, the places we can go, the foods we can eat, and the things that bring us the joy we need to keep going. We can't leave the "fear zone" by greeting our fears with even more of it. Our fears need love too. So, we can stop limiting and finally start LIVING. We need the most love when we're scared, and sometimes that's when we are too scared to ask for it or to let ourselves receive it. Love is the way (along with anything else that helps you make it through); it is the strongest medicine you can ever give yourself and others around you.

When we live in this fear and avoidance way of surviving, the symptoms can sometimes get worse. So, we need to do these things again. But instead of facing them full force, we can play first, be there and love the uncomfortable, and get our "happy dance on" to let us feel less triggered. Do it one place, one experience, one food, or one trigger at a time.

Here we get to reintroduce the things we have been limiting, the things we have been previously advised (or self-advised) to fear and avoid. Sometimes, when our symptoms get big, we begin to retract and don't want to face those things for fear of making them worse or getting the reaction we did in the past. For example, eating dairy or gluten; entering a noisy restaurant, grocery store, or place with bright lights or strong smells; driving a car; going back to work; going on a date; or taking part in a social activity. It's like when someone goes on an elimination diet (naturopath visitors know exactly what I am talking about)—you remove the foods that might be causing your symptoms, then slowly reintegrate certain foods to see how your body responds. The only difference here is that you are not trying to see how your body responds because you already know how it has been responding. That is the problem here. Your brain has linked the stimuli with inducing that response. Studying psychology taught me something.

Do you remember Pavlov's dogs? In an 1897 experiment, dogs were eventually trained to salivate whenever a bell rang. Pavlov started the experiment by ringing the bell, then feeding the dogs. After a while, the dogs expected food whenever they heard the bell. Soon, the dogs would salivate whenever hearing the bell, regardless of whether there was food or not.

This classical conditioning is exactly what's been happening in our brains. We conditioned ourselves to expect the worst will happen based on past bad experiences. For example, I went to a noisy restaurant, felt overstimulated, and my head pain got worse. Then it happened again. So, noisy places and my head hurting and feeling overstimulated and unwell have been linked. This conditioning also happens with food. I ate something that caused an adverse reaction. Because it happened more than once, I have now linked that particular food with being the cause of this reaction and symptom in my body. My brain and body have begun to expect this response will always happen.

Thus, we need to unlink the reaction to the stimulus (or the place, food, or experience). Or simply bring our four-step process to the fear that is present so that the next time we do the thing, eat the thing, or are in that environment, we don't have quite as big of a response. Moving into a more playful state, alchemizing the fear, and letting our heart take the energy from a fearful to loving inner space can support the brain and nervous system to head into homeostasis and no longer react the same way it did. This new response reaffirms that the thing we desire is possible or that we can actually do that thing and are going to be more willing to do it again. Our brain and body are needing to learn not to respond to those things. But instead of focusing on the symptoms, our goal here is to not pay attention to them. We must simply bring love into them.

I know this part can be challenging. If it is, don't think you're doing it wrong.

The last chapter and the third step of play are always here to help you integrate so this process feels easier and more fun! So, if this gets you too much in your head, breathe into your heart and skip to the fun part as much as you need before "doing the thing."

This approach is like when you deal with a child's temper tantrum or when you are training a dog. In these examples, you don't focus on the tantrum or what the dog is doing wrong. You place your focus and attention on all the positive behaviors or responses occurring, and you celebrate all the little steps in the direction of the desired behavior. Say the dog finally sits or stays. Celebrate it! You are so proud of your pup for learning this new trick. And like your dog, you, too, are going to be doing the same—and there are lots of new tricks ahead of you! It's time to remind your brain (and your dog) that this action is the new response to the command.

This action reinforces it, which keeps it happening that way. We are doing the same.

Whenever you speak to your fear with love, the brain's negativity bias isn't as present. Each time we have a new positive experience, we can celebrate and believe that the next time will be even easier, then the next time, and so on, until how we wanted to feel becomes the new norm. We are actively choosing to flip the switch to focus on the positive shifts and what we want to happen rather than the responses our brain and our neurotransmitters are used to.

So, when you're surrounded by something that would at one time trigger a symptom, you take yourself through the four steps and your brain eventually learns to respond less to the trigger. Instead of feeling activated by the trigger, it starts feeling more FUN and freeing to be able to do what you always wanted to while learning how to cultivate safety inside of you in the midst of that trigger.

Love, acceptance, and PLAY is enough to calm the storm, or in this case, the fear or trigger.

Doing this repeatedly eventually gives our brain and body the message. This is where repetition, consistency, and compassion come in. Your brain may want to stay on the merry-go-round because that's what it's gotten used to. Because new can be scary sometimes. Keep focusing on the new story and desired experiences you are creating whenever the trigger arises. And if you forget, be compassionate. Compassion will change that response just as well. Only fear will keep the loop spinning. Love that fear too, and let it change you.

Your brain and your body are changing one day, one step, and one triggering experience at a time. This in itself changes the trigger from being a bad and scary thing to being exciting, because it's the opportunity to change your brain and body's response! And to simply have fun instead.

This process is called flooding, a.k.a. "desensitization or exposure therapy." You are facing your fears, and the way you do that is not by facing them all at the same time. You (as someone who is sensitive to a lot of things) are learning how to desensitize your brain to them, which happens by adding in your alternative responses (the feeling tools that shift the response into something new). You are consciously choosing to start with a trigger, then trying a new one when that response is no longer as triggering.

In case this psychology and neuroscience mumbo jumbo has been a bit much for you, pause and play. Head to the Resources (https://www.mindbodysoulmiracles.com/eat-play-love) and watch the YouTube video of the song "Start of Something New." (Because it is!)

Have a sing, have a laugh, and get ready.

New is possible, and you get to have it while facing those fears and feeling less scared as you do.

I will guide you through some examples of this in my own journey—how I did it, what I started with, and what became possible because of this way of healing. Every moment was a chance to choose and create a new story.

"If we wait until we are ready, we'll be waiting the rest of our lives" is a great reminder and quote by Lemony Snicket. Remember, perfection is never the goal anymore. You will know it's time, even when you are not quite "ready," so take the next step.

These are the spaces, places, and experiences where we need LOVE the most to feel safe and able to do them and experience them again. Be gentle with your fears, as they are asking for and going to need all the love you have to give and play that will guide the way.

Moving through fears with love IS the most loving, rewiring, and rewarding way forward. It gets to be as simple as that, yet that in itself isn't always so simple.

It can be hard to choose love and move through our biggest fears with love as our medicine. So, remember to ask for and allow yourself to receive loving support in the areas where your fear is biggest. This is how connection comes in. You get to have more connection from here on out, even if for now that is in the form of a coach, therapist, healer, or guide. It helps us break down the fear one moment, one experience, and one part at a time until we can face it all while being able to breathe and stay present (and more playful) in the moment.

A good way of checking in with yourself is to notice if you're breathing. If you dive deep into something new (a.k.a. facing your trigger) and stop breathing, that is normally a clue you have gone too far and might need a slower, more supportive and loving approach where you can break it down into manageable steps before you take the leap.

Sometimes we need someone to hold us while we are very much in the fear until it lessens so we can face it in an easier way. You don't need to face it all, or even part of it alone. That's what partners, coaches, and communities are for. Ask for help or get a coach. They are a big part of what makes this FUN and what holds you in the moments and in the vision of what's ahead. They will help you so you don't run into the fear of doing it wrong or the fear of doing too much at once. They will keep reminding you of your why and the point of it all, even when you stumble and fall. They will continue to hold you in the certainty of where you are headed. They, too, believe in you.

We want this part to be slow and steady with fast and effective results. Turtle rules RULE here. Seriously, slow and steady wins this race. You don't need to go at someone else's pace or feel like you're behind and need to catch up. This is your pace, this is your life, this is your journey, and you know you best. I trust you. Can you? Be gentle with this part. Go as fast or as slow as truly honors you.

So, how does this look in action?

I like to use the terms I learned in teaching: the "growth zone" (growth mindset anyone?) and the "zone of proximal development."

There is our **comfort zone**, or where we are currently. We are not facing our fears or doing the things that trigger us.

Then there is the **danger zone**. We don't want to go there just YET. This is too far, too much, too fast. If it goes well here, then GREAT! But if we create another loop de loop and flood our brain with fear, it may feel too scary to try this or be faced with this trigger again. So, we want to do our best to go beyond the comfort zone yet not far enough to activate that part of our brain that screams danger!

So, where are we aiming? **The magical unicorn zone.**

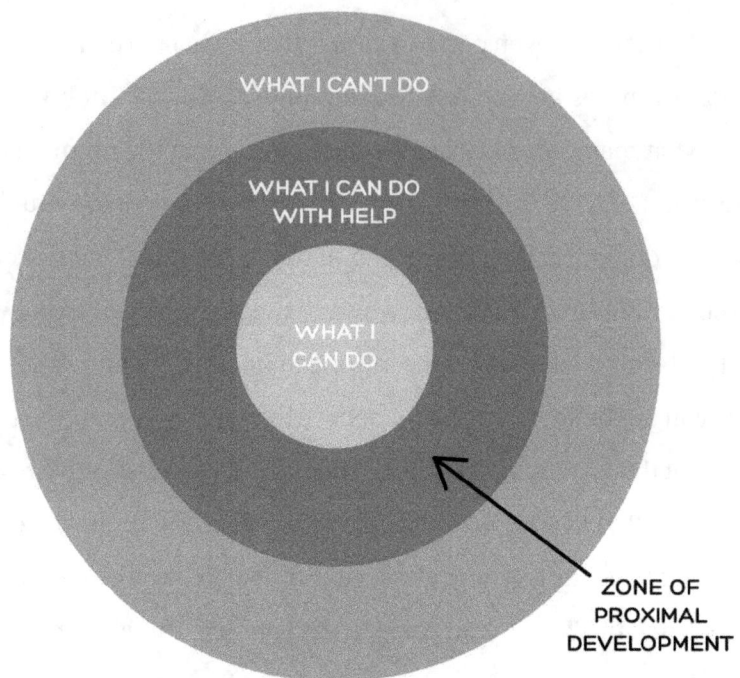

Well, that's what I like to call it. But you can call it what you want. A note: unicorns are not for everyone (and let that be okay for our people-pleasing tendencies!). This is also the **growth zone**. It's where the rewiring, relearning, and new responses are formed. It's where the MAGIC happens! This is also where the FUN happens.

The zone of proximal development is beyond what you can currently do on your own but is what you can do with help. When you have someone guiding you who has been there before, it allows you to go further faster and to do more than you can on your own. When we have a guide by our side, the danger zone becomes less dangerous. Think of it as wearing a life jacket while learning to swim. We can swim into the deep end safely because we know we will be okay, we'll keep floating, and we'll keep moving forward.

Before I share some of my examples of "rewiring" and meeting the fears with love, I want to remind you that all our journeys are different yet the same.

We may have different fears and triggers, but we all just want to feel safe and loved, to have human connection and not be stuck in our fears, and to be present. Presence is going to be the tool that we come back to if all other tools aren't working. Can you simply be here with the experience rather than resist it? If so, we can also invite acceptance into it.

Before I start, I want to explain a bit about my process because for me, most of my challenges were chronic, meaning they were present all day, every day. Some of the rewiring was simply blasting myself with love and doing the joyful, playful things, and sometimes, I even let music bring in those happy hormones and neurotransmitters by starting and ending my days with my visualizations and play. The key was also bringing in these steps when I was in excruciating pain or triggered. I would pause the fearful or worrisome thought and get back into the present moment, feel the love and acceptance I was needing, and do something fun just for me. I would remind myself that **I am not that story, then I'd keep believing in the new one I was creating**.

This helped shift the pain in the moment, and I started noticing some triggers or stimuli dissolving and no longer causing the same pain or sensitivity they once had. We start here when our challenges feel chronic because shifting the brain to be less sensitive and reactive in general is going to help us then begin the specific trigger training from a calmer, more connected and safer place within. (Think training like training the dog yet again, except this time, it's you!)

THE PAIN

I am going to start by sharing how I rewired my brain when it came to pain because this was the symptom that got triggered all the time with every single thing. I've already shared that I was sensitive to light, sound, smells, emotions, and people, because all people have emotions (including me—I have many!). Pain was my main day-to-day complaint at the time. Whatever I did, I was in pain. I would both wake up and go to bed with a headache or migraine. And if I or someone else had a lot of feelings, especially a lot of stress, the pain would always increase and get worse for me. So, I needed to wake up and go to bed by using my four-step process and tools—by starting my day with songs that brought me into that loving place, by sharing my joy and dreams out loud, and by visualizing and experiencing all the LOVE feelings. And in the moments that triggered a bigger pain response, I needed the love and acceptance tools even more! I needed to be with this with my full open heart rather than bring in the fear of "when will this finally stop?"

I started feeling empowered in moments when I once felt helpless and like nothing I did worked or could shift it. I started to notice that when I was in the feeling of how I wanted to be, seeing future possibilities, and feeling them as if they were here now, my head wouldn't feel quite as painful. So, what does this look like?

Example: I'm in a coffee shop, and the lights and the noise of other people are making my headache worse. I pause and breathe. I then consciously choose to imagine my future feeling and vision or I start to remember the funny show I watched on TV. I might choose to sing and be here fully, realizing I can focus on the fun that is already here. I tap into what brings me the most joy, love, and peace within. I start to tell a new story in my head while opening myself to loving and accepting this moment as it is. Knowing myself and what elicits that "high vibe, high loving" feeling, I choose to see myself in the future. I am out on a Sunday morning, enjoying a beautiful walk with my partner and our kiddos, who we just love, adore, and are grateful to have in our life. I can hear the birds chirping, and I can feel how connected we are and how full my heart is every single day.

This is the feeling I get to quickly when imagining this life and vision as if it is happening for me right now. Therefore, my brain feels like it is because my heart feels FULL, and I flood myself with oxytocin and all the happy hormones and neurotransmitters, and my brain gets a new message. Sometimes the pain diminishes or goes away, other times it looks or feels like nothing has happened, yet the brain is forming a new loop so the next time may be different. Both are valid. Both are okay.

The change that occurred was my not noticing the pain quite as much and remembering that repetition and consistency in these moments are key. Eventually, I stopped feeling it altogether. My brain became less sensitive in general, so even when triggers like a noisy place or a big emotion (felt by me or by another) were present, my brain was already getting used to feeling safe, feeling calm, and not needing to respond. This is how the daily practice of getting into the "feel good" feelings changes the brain at the source, creating a healthier loop so the symptoms simply decrease on their own, which is the goal here. But I want you to know that it's not about focusing on whether it's working or not, it's shifting to simply trusting that it IS and making having fun with it your goal. Know that the changes ARE taking place in your body by being in your heart and each moment fully.

So, if you have chronic, everyday symptoms or feelings, start by implementing what we practiced in the last two chapters without needing to focus on the triggers.

Just like training your pup, it's not about focusing on the problem but simply celebrating when there is a win. The win can be you no longer focusing on a symptom and being present in that moment. The win can also be you noticing that you didn't notice something that you used to. The win can be you realizing your headache is now a five rather than a ten on the pain scale. Every movement in a more loving (and less sensitive) direction is proof that what you're doing is working and that your brain and body have been learning new healthy and happier ways.

PERIOD PROBLEMS

Okay, so you may have noticed that I shared an example that REALLY resonated for me. Back to the basics, a.k.a. babies. Something that was a big issue for me most of my life, and especially after my brain injury, was my menstrual cycle. When I was young, I always experienced extreme pain at the same time every month. I felt like I was in labor, and I didn't know how to make this pain go away.

But I was also happy once I got my period because it meant that my dream of one day being pregnant and becoming a mom was possible, and that in itself brought me hope, joy, and excitement. Thus, when I stopped getting my period after my brain injury, I was really scared about what might not happen. I feared that the thing I most desired—becoming a mother—would never occur. Dealing with the constant stress of living with the symptoms of a brain injury caused my cycle to stop. It was suspected that I had polycystic ovarian syndrome (PCOS) and a bunch of other labels associated with amenorrhea. Just like joy was absent in my life, my cycle was too. It was gone. Every month would come, but my period wouldn't.

There was a moment for me years and years later in that journey when my therapist asked me to visualize. Instead of continuing to talk about or keep focusing on the fear that my dream might not happen, she asked me to address this fear in a different way. She told me to focus on what I wanted. She prompted me to envision myself surrounded by babies and children. That was my first taste of this magic. It was the flooding again—flooding my brain, my body, my ovaries, my fallopian tubes, my nervous system, my heart, and my pituitary gland with LOVE, love for these babies and for my getting to be with them in my joy. My heart and the power of this love was enough to remind my fears that they aren't as powerful as the dream. I could feel the shift, and I had a newfound sense of hope in "what could be," even though I hadn't been getting my period.

Guess what? It came back! Kind of like the childhood song about the cat that came back the very next day. Now, it didn't come back the very next day, but it did when it felt ready. And then it did again the next month. It wasn't hiding anymore, and it became more consistent than it had been in the four years since my accident. The return of my cycle was celebrated by my family and friends! Apparently, we'd talked about periods quite openly and always had! I remember there being a chain reaction group chat in my circle of people who cheered and were overjoyed about me getting my period again. It is the celebration of every little (or big) win that allows us to keep noticing and welcoming the shifts, one month or moment at a time.

WANTING SLEEP, SLEEP, AND MORE SLEEP

The ongoing, ever-present fatigue was much like a cozy blanket that was always there, making me just want to stay cocooned while doing absolutely nothing. I wanted to go to sleep whenever I could, even after a day of not doing very much. I finally began feeling a bit better after a month or so of continuously feeling the elevated emotions and practicing my visualizations of where I wanted to go and remembering how I felt during my "feel-good" moments. The more I played, the more energy I had. These "feeling" tools and "stay and play" priority were the exact medicine I needed to shift from feeling sleepy to feeling alive and awake, and noticing those moments more than the sleepy ones. It was time to start stretching my capacity to be present, to be awake, and to actually begin doing things.

I wasn't working full time because of the fatigue (along with the other associated things like the cognitive challenges and pain). It was hard to stay present and alert for a long time. And it was time to start increasing this capacity. So, when I felt tired, I would go to my happy and loving place and do more visualizations while focusing on the moments I was feeling joy, love, and pride. I noticed there was more energy here when those emotions were too.

I would visualize working in a job I loved, being in a relationship, being around children I loved, and **feeling energized, alive, and more present than ever.** That thought energized me, and I soon knew it was almost time to increase my ability to work a little more and be present with people for longer periods of time.

I wasn't yet ready to do things like this sustainably, so I needed to keep imagining them, which was all so my brain could believe it was real for me in the moment. Slowly, I noticed that I would feel awake longer one day than I had the day before. This was the WIN. I needed to keep focusing on these moments when the energy expanded longer and to keep celebrating the shifts. Every day that I did, it reminded me of what was possible, and I was then able to stay awake even longer the next week, month, and so on. This is the goal here. Not to get down on ourselves when we don't see improvement or a change, we must simply notice and celebrate where and when we do.

We need to set a new expectation that is the opposite of the one we used to expect and focus on. Now, we are excited every time we have more energy! And now, we have even more energy from that excitement and are actually able to do things that we once thought weren't possible!

TIME TO WORK (AND PLAY) AGAIN!

Remember, for me, babies helped me tap into the LOVE feeling quickly, so I got to experience spending time with a baby I loved. This truly was a beautiful way to consistently flood my brain and my whole being with love, oxytocin, and happy hormones.

That said, being with a baby was the perfect rewiring opportunity because it also brought in some challenges for me—staying awake for extended periods of time, being present, remembering things, and crying all used to stimulate pain. So, being around a human who cried from time to time (like babies do) was a beautiful opportunity to heal this response with love (and snuggles and fun little songs and books!).

Once my brain was in a better place, I chose to move from being a part-time babysitter and nanny for a sweet little one-year-old (something I had just gotten back into after not working for quite some time) to full time instead. I was rewiring my brain around the pain, fatigue, people, emotions, and working again. Mostly, it was my play. It warmed my heart. I had been off work for a really long time, so it was hard for me to try it again. I hadn't really done anything for a full day while feeling good since my brain injury. Full days meant feeling bad and just needing to collapse and sleep as soon as I could.

It was a perfect rewiring opportunity for me because that sweet little one and I were constantly living in love, so whenever a symptom appeared, this love and my tools helped me shift the response. I now had something to focus on that brought me joy, meaning, and purpose.

Our purpose is sometimes taken away when we are sick. Hence, finding our purpose again is a big healer and can help bring in the hope of what can be. Sometimes we need to distract ourselves and get back into our heart when a symptom is really big. The connection I had to this human whom I loved so much helped me to stay in my heart, and this feeling of love, connection, and play supported me big time, even when I was afraid or a symptom got bigger.

Something I want to remind you of is that healing is not linear. Healing is rarely a straight line; it can sometimes be full of uphill or curvy roads with maybe a pothole or two. And other times, it's smooth cruising down the road for miles. Simply put, it's a journey. You've got to keep believing in your healing! Even when it looks like it isn't working, you can still believe and remember that it is. Before I completely shifted a trigger response, I sometimes experienced the response in a bigger way than I ever had. That does not have to happen, but if it does, know it can mean you are ready to level up!

In these moments, I was reminded of the phrase, "Instead of why me? Try me!" I would remind myself that even though the symptom came up bigger than ever this time, it didn't mean I was getting worse and not getting better. In these moments, I needed to remind myself about what was possible, what wins already happened, then ground myself in the knowing of what was to come, even if it felt like this symptom was the opposite of that reality. Trusting and having faith is important. Both believing in and holding on to the feeling are going to keep our perspective and knowingness that we ARE shifting, even when we may not see it.

SEEING THE LIGHTS

One of the symptoms I used to experience was that every sensation was louder to my head than it actually was. So, I wanted to rewire my brain and not keep expecting this response to happen when I went to public places like stores, restaurants, or anywhere where there were lights and noise. As I write this, I am in a coffee shop filled with bright light, and ambient music is playing loudly from every direction. There are people present—conversing, working, being, and doing. Because I was scared of this type of situation once and still focusing on my potential response, I started by "getting my FUN on" (on my own at home) first. Before going to a bright and noisy place, I would play some music and picture myself doing the things and having the experience I wanted to feel.

For example, I would bring loving feelings and dream experiences into my visualizations to amplify the feeling. I would picture myself at a restaurant that I love with my friends and them sharing with me all about the best things that have been happening for them lately. Or I'd play the "What Makes Me Happy game" to amp up the feel-good feels. Specifically, I would picture myself in situations that do make me happy, like sitting down with my friends who are getting married and them telling me all the fun stuff they have been planning for their special day. This integrated the feeling of love and the feeling of being connected. Being so focused on this visualization and fun, I no longer focused on the sounds, the lights, or anything else that used to ignite my symptoms. Sometimes I simply visualized myself sitting there smiling when my favorite song came on, being happy to be there and feeling fantastic! (Because coffee shops, music, friends and yummy coffee really are some of the things that make me HAPPY!)

Therefore, whenever I went to a restaurant (or store or loud or light-filled place), I had now formed a new expectation or envisioned a new reality and response or simply brought myself out of the expected "fight or flight" by being primed by play and in the parasympathetic nervous system instead. I wouldn't even notice the trigger anymore. In hind-sight, I would realize that the pain or the sensation wasn't as big, and sometimes, that it wasn't even there anymore.

The difference is where we place our attention and focus. It's difficult not to focus on the problems at first when it feels hard to engage with people we love, feel safe within our mind, body and soul, and be inside the place when we feel like we are constantly in pain. Love and accept any fears that have come up here. The next time you do it, it will be easier. It was for me until suddenly I was able to be present with my people, and I realized the lights weren't screaming at me anymore. (Which made me want to happy dance!) I didn't even notice them and instead felt grateful and full of love and joy to simply be there. When I forgot about my surroundings and focused on being with the people and feelings I loved, the rest went away.

VROOM VROOM, LET'S GET BACK IN THE FAST LANE

Now for the more specific things to rewire around and the triggers or fears to consciously choose to move through, one at a time. This process can be extremely challenging and can cause a lot of fear to surface. (The story I am about to tell you was not from the "I can love and accept my fears fully place" or four-step process.) Some of the steps were present, like visualizing and elevating my full-heart feelings. For me, a big one was driving. I had a really slow processing speed and actually noticed it become faster with the continued practice of changing my brain (the trauma loop) and the constant flooding of myself with love and elevated emotions and fun music. Yet even so, I still had a lot of fear about driving fast. I had been stuck in the slow lane for quite some time. I hadn't driven on the highway since my accident, as I felt that my brain was too slow to keep up. It was the same feeling for me when it came to following conversations. It felt like I was in another country and everyone else was speaking a language I couldn't understand.

Driving and keeping up with conversations were the places my brain was ready to change, and I had to train my capacity to face them bit by bit. With driving, I would prepare my body with feel-good feelings and visualize myself on the highway, driving with my favorite songs playing, feeling good, feeling calm, feeling alive. And then when I felt like I was able to start facing this fear, I would get on the highway and then off at the next exit. I was still terrified. I could feel my nervous system ramp up with fear, but I knew that this was my chance to shift this response. So, I would pull over, visualize something that really brought me back to the present moment with love, then get back into my heart. Afterward, I would do something really fun, really loving, then go on with my day.

Then on another day, I would do it again, and I'd notice that I wasn't quite as scared as I had been the time before. I had a new baseline. I loved playing music because it automatically brought me into those elevated emotions. I would play songs that brought me into my joy and play. I often played Taylor Swift, which reminded me of the freedom I felt when I got to drive on my own for the first time after passing my driver's test. Anyone else remember bobbing their head to "Fearless" while driving with the windows down and feeling freer than ever before?! This is the feeling I would come back to, and that song would easily let me get there.

With this new baseline, I would drive a little longer the next time and maybe get off at the fourth exit. Still feeling ramped up, I would keep driving with my favorite songs playing until I found my calm, and I would celebrate this win—saying yes to the highway and simply trying was a win in and of itself. The first time I got on the highway, it was hard for me to breathe—this was close to my danger zone—so that's why I got off quickly because breathing is the priority. But the next few times got easier until I even allowed myself to have fun with it!

I was eventually able to merge onto the highway with ease and felt free driving on the highway whenever I pleased. I felt confident. My brain felt laser-focused, sharp, and fast, and I realized just how far I had come. I would get giddy with excitement and feel proud of myself every time I was on the highway because the shifts I experienced here proved to me just how possible it is to change our brain, shift our fear into new possibilities, and do things that we thought we might never be able to again. This gave me the confidence to go for more!

But first, I needed to believe in me, my body, and that I could do hard things, big things, small things, and even the simplest of things, at my own pace, filled with play, love, and acceptance of where I am at and what my next step with love would be.

You see, going too fast all at once from zero to one hundred is a sure-fire way to end up in the danger zone where every part of you feels like it's on red alert. Think bright neon letters flashing DANGER, DANGER!

Let me share with you the story of when I entered a danger zone and tried to face a bunch of fears all at once. It's funny in retrospect, and I have a lot of respect for the impatient part of me that just wanted to have it all (like now!) even though on the inside, it was hard to breathe and hard to see that it might have been too much to face too soon, especially without support.

DATING, RELATING, AND HIGHWAY 401

I had already rewired a lot of my beliefs, thoughts, and responses, and I was facing a lot of the fears that once kept me stuck. It's like I got a high or a dopamine hit from knowing that all these things that were once such a problem were now possible for me, and I wanted to keep going.

The truth is, part of me always felt like I was behind on all the things in life. There was no shaking away that feeling. I think that happens when a time of our life has been characterized by being sick, by missing out, and by living in constant fear of missing out (FOMO). I remember that part, being used to the FOMO and realizing I had zero fear of missing out. I felt like missing out was a given; it was my life. I was used to it.

And an area I missed out on most was having a personal life, especially in having a partner, a boyfriend, and dating. When we are sick or have lots of symptoms we're managing daily, we sometimes stop doing certain activities altogether. Dating was one of those for me. I had a lot of reasons for doing so, and I'm sure you might have something in your life that is similar. It can feel hard to be around the people you love, who love you when you are sick. It can be hard to be present, to actually be there and devote the energy you desire to connect with and spend time with them. And there is zero fear of rejection with those people, so imagine entering a zone where you are potentially going to be rejected.

One of my deeply held patterns and fears was rejection, especially in the dating arena. Prior to my brain injury, I hadn't had much luck or many positive experiences with men or with staying in relationships. I was always afraid that they would decide they didn't want to be with me anymore. I think this belief came from my inner child, who had a lot of fears and hurt feelings. Honestly, I think a lot of it came back to feeling like I needed to be perfect to feel and be worthy of love and receiving love.

Having a brain injury and what I felt were so many things WRONG with me meant that letting someone into my heart, my life, and my space was difficult. I felt like I had no time or energy or mental, physical, or emotional capacity for a relationship. And I feared being bad at things (sex included) and being judged by others for having a lack of experience in these areas since I had been sick and had avoided dating for a long time.

It's safe to say that I was terrified of getting back in the dating game with that possibility of being judged as inexperienced. And with the cognitive issues I was experiencing, I feared that I wouldn't be able to keep up with the conversation or have anything of value or interesting to say. I also feared that all my diet issues and my inability to be in loud places meant I'd be an inconvenience. I felt this so much that I believed I couldn't date. It felt impossible. *How could I have fun and be on a date when there were so many restrictions to where I could go and what I could do and eat?*

Once I had moved through those fears and rewired my brain around a lot of things, it felt like the only fear left was actually dating and being in a relationship. So, I was determined to face it. I am one of those people who LOVE love. I would have happily fit into the movie *Love Actually* or *The Notebook*.

Love is literally the feeling that healed me the most, but it was also the thing I was afraid of the most. During the time of falling in love with myself on this journey, I had also fallen in love with someone who came into my life. I deeply feared sharing this fact with him, thinking that he might not feel the same way. I also feared that my awkward self would come out and that my words wouldn't match my heart. I felt as if I had zero game whatsoever. And that was the exact thing I didn't want to face: people playing games when it came to dating. I wanted to skip to the relationship part because in the past, the getting into the relationship part was where I would run into difficulties.

I prepared to enter my danger zone. Dating was my "highway" I hadn't yet faced. It was finally getting safer and easier for me to drive on highways, and yet I hadn't ventured onto the biggest highway where I was living (Highway 401) or the highway of love.

I decided it would be a great idea (oops) to face the complexities of dating all at once.

To paint you a picture: I had been visualizing being in a relationship, having conversations, and it going well with me feeling confident and sexy. (Sidenote: At the time, I couldn't fully feel sexy. It's not a word I associated with myself. I'd giggle when I tried, so I knew it was something I would need to lean into more before I fully felt it.)

Despite my attempts to visualize it going well, what came next was definitely NOT that. I texted the person I was falling for, with the intention of sharing my true feelings for him and letting him know that I really wanted to explore them and share them from my heart. To be fair, I also intuitively felt that he had the same feelings for me and wanted to hear what I had to say, so I may have held some expectations here. But our connection felt scary because it wasn't something I understood logically. It was more something I felt in my soul. It felt like I sensed what he was thinking or feeling, and it felt like he connected with me on the same level too.

Meanwhile, I had also been invited to be a guest speaker out in another province which was big because it meant getting on a plane by myself for the first time in years and flying out to British Columbia. I had been visualizing this and truly felt confident about sharing my story and journey with others in the secure setting of the program that invited me. I also knew my sister would be waiting for me in BC (she lived there), and I was looking forward to that visit.

Reflecting on where I had been when I had attended that program to where I was now (able to speak to the attendees as someone who was doing so much better) added to the feeling that I was conquering all the fears on my list. I was on a roll, so the night before my big trip, I got in my car and faced the 401 (that incredibly massive, fast-paced, multiple-lane highway in the greater Toronto area), ready to proclaim my love.

Let's think about this for a second: Attempting to drive on the 401 was one big fear in itself. Maybe doing that on its own, then pausing to play, rest, and simply honor this next step for my nervous system and my brain/body would have been the best and most loving next step. But instead, I faced that AND I faced my biggest fear of all: intimacy.

I had never been in this kind of situation, and I hadn't felt like this before with anyone or felt this called to share such a big thing. I got to his place and felt so nervous, awkward, and anxious. I wasn't the only one. I remember us both acting like awkward teenagers at a dance, sitting at opposite ends of a room, not knowing how to be human, let alone knowing how to have a conversation about matters of love. I got tongue-tied and blurted out my feelings, not exactly as I had intended or envisioned, but I was pretty clear about what I was trying to say. It was like I had faced my fear and flopped right into awkward land.

My big, courageous, bold proclamation of love did NOT go exactly as I hoped or visualized. I ended up running away, feeling scared, rejected, and like my feelings weren't totally reciprocated. The alarms had already gone off—my fight-or-flight responses were reactivated and there to play the game. The rejection was a cue to my full body that I was in the DANGER ZONE where it was not safe, and I needed to GET OUT OF THERE. FAST.

So, I drove back home (back on the highway, bringing in even more fear after a triggering experience). Once I arrived, I was barely able to sleep. Then, not many hours later, I was headed to the airport to go on my first solo trip since my brain injury journey with barely any sleep and heightened emotions.

I remember crying at the airport, feeling like I was back in high school when boys didn't like me, and like I might be alone forever. Talk about being intense and dramatic, but that's what can happen when we get re-triggered and the response is bigger than our ability to remind ourselves that we are SAFE and not in danger anymore. My brain kept replaying the loop and the stories that no longer served me, and I needed my tools to get back "home" to me (and my homeostasis within) before facing another fear again.

Why am I telling you this story? Well, because a) it's kinda funny. And although maybe not smart, I also want to celebrate my courage and bravery to do the things that scared me most, albeit very awkwardly and imperfectly. And b) this example really honors any learning journey. It's a beautiful example of knowing that you might not get it right all the time, especially on the first try, but that's to be expected. And sharing is where we can learn from another's missteps and thus break it into smaller, more manageable steps instead of "face it all and FAST," which can re-trigger or traumatize us, rather than "rewire the brain" or nervous system in positive ways.

Sometimes, as much as we desire something, the reality that transpires may be far from what we expected. And every single time, finding safety, love, acceptance, and feeling okay in these moments is the learning and win in and of itself. And on this learning journey, I can now celebrate that, and unlike in this previous example, I can now date (and be in a long-term relationship) where the love is mutual while breathing and having fun, which is an area that has definitely evolved and has been full of enjoyment!

My sharing this story can help you experience your own personal shifts and learning, possibly with fewer falls than I had. Instead of doing what I did, you can learn from it. This experience can help you understand what triggers are BIG and which ones to break down into steps and play some more. That way you can face your fears one bit and experience at a time. If dating is a trigger for you, you get a bit more support in learning to feel these fears fully, releasing any limiting beliefs, hurt, or pain in the way. Then try getting back in the game and doing it for the fun of it rather than with so much high pressure or attachment to an outcome. But also remember that with anything that really matters to us in life, we will never be 100 percent ready, so don't wait to start or try. Keep stepping out of that comfort zone in a way that feels loving to you and meets you at your edge, rather than jumping straight off the cliff head (or heart) first.

And mostly, I want you to know that if you get into the DANGER ZONE, it's not something you need to shame, blame, or get mad at yourself for. Lean into self-compassion, dial up that LOVE and ACCEPTANCE, and get back to you, to what brings you joy, calm, love, and peace. And keep taking those four steps forward with you.

Your journey is specific to you, and so are your triggers. Break them down one bit at a time and know that if you hit the danger zone, you can find your fun and get back into the feeling you desire and start again (when and only when you feel ready-ish to start again).

I know that when we get really triggered or are in the rewiring mode and four-step process, especially if we hit the DANGER ZONE, we can have trouble remembering these steps and tools. We may need a quick and easy win to focus on—to bring us back that light! This is why I talk about FUN. Of course, we can bring in a mental reminder like a word or pattern interrupt, like your favorite TV show or music video that makes you laugh. Keep your "code word" or something that ignites a giggle for the moments you need that re-shift and reminder you can stop taking this all so darn seriously!

Remember, if none of this works for you, I simply want you to PLAY. There is never too much play. And because you may need to keep telling yourself this, just like Trix cereal, **PLAYTIME isn't just for kids.** This popular (anonymous) saying reminds us that "the creative adult is the child who survived." *Let the fun of your inner child live on.* And true to that, allow this beautiful side of your inner child to come out and play—into adulthood!

Let's take all this learning and keep turning up the PLAY by taking action on one fear and desired new experience and "big why" at a time.

TAKEAWAY & P L A Y

Before we begin, I want you to pause and breathe. You might be excited or a little scared to start the things you have been avoiding or not doing for a while.

Your fears are welcome, and we want to make this as loving and FUN as it can be.

Make a list of all the things, places, foods, or experiences you avoid.

My examples: dairy, gluten, driving long distances or at night, going back to work

Once you have made your list, organize it in the order of what is the easiest thing to reintroduce (to face) to the hardest. Think "thing that brings up the least fear" to "thing that brings up the most fear."

Now, make your "four-step process" even clearer and readily available by printing out the PDF on the Resources page of my website: https://www.mindbodysoulmiracles.com/eat-play-love. You can put down examples of "ways to play" so they are readily available, or you can get creative, listen to those intuitive

TAKEAWAY & PLAY

nudges, and simply have fun! You can follow along the four steps and then get into action.

- What is the new experience you want to create?
- How would you like to feel when you try these experiences again?
- Note: You can also go back to the meditation in the last chapter and keep practicing visualizing until it becomes a natural thing for you to do on your own—before, during, or after facing a fearful situation, experience, or trigger, if this method of visualization resonates more than the steps mentioned here. Either way, you've got this!

Now, it's go time!

Time to take imperfect action. Take action and repeat steps one through four as much as you want and need!

Start at the smallest thing that triggers you and bring your tools, four steps, and elevated expectations and desired feelings to it, one at a time.

Start small and keep doing it until it is part of your everyday life.

TAKEAWAY & PLAY

Until that playful resting state is your new baseline or you feel like love, acceptance, and welcoming it all is easy when facing the new. This is beautiful too!

Then, when you are ready for more, start small with the next item and experience on your list.

Remember, ask for support. Consider doing these exercises with friends or family supporting you to talk through them, to play with, to dialogue around the fear with, and to help you visualize. This may be even easier if you have a coach to guide you and celebrate alongside you and hold you when the fear may be big. You may need to break it down together! I didn't get extra support at the time and was convinced that I knew what I was doing, but I was rushing and fearing my fear through it a lot. You won't have to do that here. Truthfully, I wish I had sought out additional support. Let yourself be guided here. You will be grateful you did!

And don't forget to CELEBRATE! Being in the game is enough to count as a WIN.

TAKEAWAY & P L A Y

I see you.

I applaud you.

I welcome your fears, and I trust you will be guided toward what you need, with love, acceptance, and so much fun and connection.

I love you for your courage, your consistency, and for showing up and doing the damn thing, especially when you're scared.

This IS living, and you're finally doing it again! You CAN do this.

Don't stop believing! Remember that sometimes that little voice singing the timeless hit by Journey is actually you. I'm also singing for you and with you.

And last but not least, keep breathing. Hand on heart: one breath, one miracle, one shift at a time.

Chapter 13

THE GUT-BRAIN CONNECTION

Do you carry a lot of rules around what you *can* and *can't* eat?

I did too. I had trouble letting go of the strict guidelines I was given (prescribed) when it came to eating because of the brain-gut connection.

I had so many symptoms that came from this silly loop of the gut affecting the brain and the brain affecting the gut. In fact, I had a whole host of illnesses associated with it: irritable bowel syndrome (IBS), leaky gut, constipation, candida, food sensitivities, small intestinal bacterial overgrowth (SIBO), and the best of the bunch—parasites (ew!).

But I think the biggest factor was my fear around what happened to me when I ate those "inflammatory" foods. I was still experiencing brain fog, plus bloating and constipation were a constant in my life until I started learning the tools to calm myself and my nervous system, which calmed my gut too.

But—and there was a big BUT here—whenever I would attend my appointments and was asked about my gut (among other things), I would also re-experience the fears and the feelings in my body. Those uncomfortable, icky, and anxiety-provoking feelings that resided in my gut were back.

Yet a new feeling began revealing itself. I wasn't used to feeling like I knew that something was happening beyond what I could logically understand. It was as if all this gut-brain talk didn't feel aligned with my gut feeling. Like all I had just learned about healing went against looking at the gut and seeing it as the problem (or even *as* a problem).

Something was telling me that the solution to healing my gut and my brain was *trusting my gut.*

Let's talk about this for a second.

We are often taught as children to listen to the teacher, to follow the rules, and to not break the mold (I also developed a mold sensitivity!), but those are hard lessons to let go of. Throughout my time of engaging in play as a way to heal, I was still seeking support from my team of practitioners. I feel beyond grateful for the ways they held me, guided me, and supported me.

Yet there came a time when it was time to let go.

Remember the quote "When the student is ready, the teacher will appear"? Well, the second part of the quote is "When the student is really ready, the teacher will disappear."

I had been a student of my body, my mind, and my healing for quite some time, and somewhere along the way I learned that I was my own teacher too.

And some of the things I learned were teaching me to keep following the way of play and to not keep focusing on the problem, the next protocol, or what could go wrong.

And this felt scary to me. This brought on fear that I couldn't trust myself or trust this new way over the way that the people I trusted and had learned alongside knew.

I had a new sense of knowing, but it was unknown (and new) to me.

But before I had it, I played with a lot of questions. A lot of curiosity led to this feeling.

So, let me share more with you because you might be wondering, like I did, how to approach your curiosity and this new sense of knowing and trusting yourself and what feels true for you.

Although I had been singing my way through healing my body (hence the fun new playful way), I still carried a bit of the tune that felt comfortable and oh so familiar! (My inner "people pleaser" was still trying to say hey!)

I had been noticing so many shifts in the direction toward what I wanted and how I wanted to feel. And so many of my symptoms had gone away.

But at the same time, I was still fearful of reintroducing the foods that had been on my list of foods to avoid. Yet this new awareness, this new approach to healing and facing the fears slowly convinced me that it was possible to also change my brain and body's reaction to the food (i.e., the triggers in this case). I had been seeing a bunch of specialists who were still hyper focused on this gut-brain connection—on healing my gut to support the rest of my healing because there were so many things wrong with it and my digestion at the time. Amid the back and forth, I realized that while I was wholeheartedly engaged in play, in joy, and in actually living life, I didn't notice the same digestive issues I had been having for so long. In fact, they seemed nearly nonexistent. And I had stopped looking at or looking for the problems.

It was only at my appointments when I was asked about my symptoms that this feeling of "I'm not feeling well" kept coming back. And somehow, despite being attuned to that inner knowing, I kept returning. I kept doubting this inner knowing and questioning my self-trust, which created the loop of going back to feeling the same way I used to. It was time to stop going back and to finally fully move forward into the new, and to do it in a way that was much more fun.

But my inner child and her performing, people-pleasing, and perfectionistic tendencies were still trying to stay—totally countering the "stay and play" way.

Around this time I had also been seeing a new practitioner who was adamant about me going on a new diet, the low FODMAP diet, to help treat SIBO and the other digestive issues I was having. For the first time, however, I felt icky about this idea (which is the only way I can describe it). It was my first experience having my intuition tell me that something felt off. In thinking about wanting to try this new elimination diet, I felt my gut twist and turn at the thought of following one more thing and restricting myself and avoiding things AGAIN when I had finally just started a new way forward that had the total opposite effect. But I was torn when it came to my well-being because I really wanted to feel well and to not have the digestive problems.

Was I wrong in not wanting to follow what the expert was saying? Was he right? Was my new way of helping myself not going to work?

I can say with confidence that the medicine I needed was not in a protocol or in following someone else above myself. It was in the little nudge I got next.

But before I got that nudge, I started to play with life as it played with me. My curiosity arose, and I saw this as an opportunity to test out my new theory.

I tried the diet and didn't feel better; in fact, I felt anxious about whether it was going to support me. But instead of letting the anxiety win, I got curious. I asked myself how I could test it or play with it and see how I felt when a) I avoided the food, and b) I ate the food with love and without the rule of it being wrong or bad.

I remember eating something that I was told specifically not to. I immediately felt the digestive upset and issues, and I think it was even more severe because of the idea that I was breaking the rules of what I was supposed to do to feel better. Stress does affect our gut health, and there are numerous studies that show just how valuable our gut health is to our overall well-being. In fact, our gut is often referred to as our second brain. That explains the inner knowing part!

Interestingly enough, when I changed the way I viewed the food that was "off-limits" and then ate what I wanted with love and enjoyment, the response wasn't as significant. When I wasn't attaching negative emotions to food, making it mean something about myself or viewing it as bad, my body barely reacted to it.

Hmm, maybe this new way was showing me something. Maybe this new way was about finally choosing what felt true for me without needing to follow everybody else's rules and recommendations. What if I finally started to listen to myself, my own voice? What if I made and trusted my own choices?

Cue fear. The thought of trusting my own choices was pretty scary for me, if I'm being honest. My new way was the opposite of what was prescribed to me by all the practitioners I was seeing. And they were the experts, after all. But I remembered that one of the first experts I'd seen years earlier told me that I had plateaued and wouldn't get any better, and she was wrong. Maybe these other practitioners were wrong too.

So, what if I became an expert on me? What if I could create a new belief and fully jump in with both feet, putting my heart and happiness first?

That's what I did next. I let my happiness and my heart lead. I ditched the rulebook, the shoulds, and the right or wrong actions, and I finally heard ME and my truth. It felt scary. And at the same time . . . it felt FUN and extremely empowering.

I remember having a lot of questions.

"But what if I'm wrong?"

"What if I don't do this protocol and because of that, I don't get better, I don't heal?"

But healing is returning to wholeness. And my soul wanted more than anything to be in the driver's seat of my own life. Remember that I was in the passenger seat the day of my accident—well, it wasn't the first time. Metaphorically speaking, up until this point, I had been the passenger in my own life. It was finally my turn to drive.

Yet driving on a road that nobody I knew had driven on before felt fucking terrifying.

The question repeated in my head: "But what if I'm wrong?"

But there was this feeling that I couldn't fight. It was my intuition. It was my truth. I had never felt something so strong before even though I also felt fear, resistance, and that incessant question in my mind.

The loudest voice was mine, however. The loudest voice was the one inside.

And I couldn't NOT listen.

Do you ever have those moments when you have all the reasons why something makes perfect, logical sense but you just know, with every fiber of your being, that it is a no? Or you feel like there is something you want to say yes to but you can't shake that "knowing" guiding you to say no?

All the facts and the logic and the usual way of healing would have told me to stay and keep fixing, going to appointments, and managing the issues, but I knew deep in my soul and in my heart that it was time to step away and PLAY. To fully trust and follow my own fun way.

Something incredible happens when we start to have faith and a lot of fun in our lives. We trust that we're guided, even if there is still a pull to stick to what we once knew. So, when we have all these questions, we know we can ask and there will be an answer that reminds us that our truth is loud and clear. We can trust ourselves.

I had one of those moments when I was guided to a book. You see, I wasn't the only one who believed in this other way of healing—that maybe illnesses or diseases were not a problem to be fixed but were instead guiding us and our soul to whatever it was we needed to learn, needed to see, or needed to honor within ourselves. Author Louise Hay listened to her inner voice, or what she likes to call her "inner ding," and she wrote a book about this way of "healing."

In *You Can Heal Your Life*, Hay speaks of every disease as a "dis-ease" having a mental cause, something that our soul wants to know in order to come into wholeness and realignment with truth and love. This is the beginning of healing with the mind-body connection and what brought it home for me.

While reading her book, I felt called to look up the mental cause of parasites (one of the many not-so-fun gut issues I had). The thing is, I just knew. I knew I needed to look it up and to see the truth in *You Can Heal Your Life*.

The mental cause of parasites is "giving away your power." And the remedy? To be in your power and stop giving it away. It might be taking it back, yet for me, it was about trusting that I, and we, have had the power all along, and we can choose at any moment to honor it, heal and hear ourselves, and to live an empowered life—one choice at a time.

So, I was faced with a choice: I could follow the FODMAPS diet or not.

And like I said, that choice brought up so many questions. Yet my game of testing it out led me to the answers I needed to trust my choice, even if I was still a bit afraid.

My empowered choice was indeed to (as I liked to call it) FUCK THE FODMAPS. I would ditch the rules, the protocols, and even the practitioners I loved, respected, and adored because my "inner ding" was louder than any other voice. And it was calling me to make this move. I didn't know why, but I had trust in *me* in a way I never had before.

So, it was time to start actually eating the CAKE, not just collecting the ingredients and baking it.

I didn't exactly start with cake, though. I started with one "no" food at a time while realizing that eating it *with the most joy and love ever* was what I needed to do to alter my body's response so I no longer felt the way I had. And it didn't exactly happen all at once. Sometimes the symptoms still come back, but they've lessened over time.

But like the voice of my intuition being louder than my fears, *my joy* in eating these foods was louder and more *pleasurable* than the symptoms, so I stopped caring so much about them and they eventually went away. And so did the parasites. Because I couldn't care less anymore; instead, I was finally *living* and *loving* my life.

I kept trying new foods, which led to feeling confident enough to trust this new way of healing while finally saying farewell to the "fixing" way. And that also meant saying goodbye to people who had been a key part of my healing journey. These professionals were people with whom I had grown to love, lean on, and share so much of myself and my journey. It was hard to let go of what had become such a routine in my life. It is similar to letting go of the trauma expectation of expecting symptoms to keep coming back. Resistance rears its head in a big way here, and so does the knowing that it's time to let go and start anew.

Meister Eckhart, the thirteenth century philosopher and mystic said, "And suddenly you know, it's time to start something new and trust the magic of beginnings."

I was ready to believe in that magic and to trust that what awaited me would be way better than what I had been experiencing.

And that felt sad. And scary. It was in saying goodbye that I feared the "what if I'm wrong" and the feeling that I may need to justify my choices. In the end, I had to trust that when you know, you know. Even if you don't know why you know, you can trust the feeling and not have to explain it. I was learning this fact for the first time. I wanted to be able to explain myself, to apologize, and for some reason, I felt like I had to give some long explanation as to why it felt like it was time to say goodbye.

So, I brought in my handy-dandy tools to elevate my emotions in order to get ready to face the music (say goodbye to the team I loved and appreciated so much). I was living in the new way, the play way, because how I prepped for this goodbye was probably the most "Amanda" way I could: I listened to a few favorite songs and sang them loudly in my car.

It was difficult for me because up until this point, I had been living with the *High School Musical* songs of "We're All in This Together" and "Stick to the Status Quo," so it felt wrong to finally be going my own way. I pressed play and let Zac Efron inspire me. There were three songs that helped: "Breaking Free," "Bet On It," the best of them all, "Gotta Go My Own Way." (I highly recommend you google these songs to fully understand the synchronicity of this soundtrack at that time for me.)

These songs got me ready to share my truth and to trust that it was time to believe in myself and know that every person, every guide, and every team member had led me to that moment.

We know what is true for us. We know what our most aligned, truest next step is. And we know when it's time to let go and go our own way.

I was greeted that day with so much celebration and understanding. I was scared that saying goodbye would mean that I didn't appreciate them and all they did for me, but nothing could be further from the truth. I wouldn't be where I am today without them, and this next step was about me doing what I needed for me. It was time to go, to finally live, and to break free. This is where the limitless part comes in, and because of them, the world has opened up for all that is ahead, which is so much more than I had even believed was possible for me. They helped me believe and taught me that with this belief (and all these tools) that the world truly is my oyster.

And after telling one of the practitioners that it felt like time to stop our sessions, he kindly responded, "This was the whole point, Amanda. You getting better was the whole point!"

Whoa! Maybe this was the whole point!

My learning to hear myself, trust myself, find myself, and come home to "me," to make my own damn choices, to trust in my own inner knowing, and to believe in myself and my dreams was exactly the whole point.

TAKEAWAY & P L A Y

IT'S JOURNAL TIME:

Listen to your heart, listen to your inner voice, and answer it.

- What are you ready to hear?
- What is your "inner ding" asking you to do, to see, to acknowledge as your truth? (Even if it's scary, new, or not what "other people" think, believe, or want for you.)
- What songs bring you back home to you?
- What is the truth that might give you the pep in your step you need to make your move?

Your heart knows the way.

Take a step (or a skip or two!).

Don't be afraid to let go. That's how you let the new in. It might be sad and exciting all at the same time. Welcome it all and walk through the door that's opening.

Chapter 14

HOW GUACAMOLE, TEQUILA, PIZZA, AND DANCING HELPED HEAL ME

I'm sure the title of this chapter sparked some excitement in you! Who doesn't want to get healthy by indulging in these things?

Did I ever think that these would be the things that would help me get better? Definitely not.

Did I ever know that there was a fun way to find health, happiness, and true wholeness again? Also, definitely not!

This is the chapter where we finally get to have the cake, eat it, and dance around while LOVING it! Not to mention appreciating the celebration and having others join in alongside us!

This is also the chapter where we can recognize that we've made it through SO much mud and are now feeling like the LOTUS we knew was inside us all along! We'll have appreciation for the journey and the realization that we have found ourselves through it—we'll have appreciation for the ever evolving true "us."

Our recipe is coming together with so much more ease, and we are enjoying every step of the cake-making now! It turns out that the journey really is all about finding the *fun* and the *joy* in living that will help make anything work again, including our own bodies.

It's funny because this part came together when I chose to go on a week-long silent retreat that I was originally afraid to go to because all the food served was on my list of things to avoid.

I loved everything about that week! And interestingly, that week was "play" in a new and very different way. It's always fun telling people about that week because a) people can't imagine not talking for a week, and b) people can't imagine ME not talking for a week!

Both things are possible if we believe they are! (Notice the theme here once again.)

It turned out to be a lot easier than I thought, and it was the most magical and life-changing week of my life!

I remember reading a quote that said, "Silence isn't empty, it's full of answers." I read those words right after the retreat when I returned to a life of being able to speak and use technology, both things I didn't miss as much as I thought I might. You see, the silence made my "inner ding" and voice stronger and louder because I knew (without a doubt) that what I was hearing was me. I knew what felt true.

And this was a week of reintroducing a whole lot of NEW (including new foods, especially dessert!).

Everything about the silent retreat was simply wonderful: the yoga, the meditating, the sharing in the experiences of others and knowing that even without talking, we were there to support one another with love, kindness, and compassion.

What is funniest of all, however, is that this week will forever be remembered because of the food! Well, for me, at least. Before going to the retreat, I had been on that never-ending list of strict diets and "don't eat these foods" in order to help me heal my gut. This was the beginning of eating the FODMAPS because at the retreat, the food was all vegetarian, meaning ALL THE FODMAPS would be served!

Back to the fun part! (The "fuck the FODMAPS" part!)

My initial plan at the retreat was to slowly reintegrate some foods, but I was still hesitant to try them. Then it just hit me that I didn't care about the rules anymore. I was ready to stop going at a slow and steady pace because I truly felt ready. The fear wasn't there anymore.

I basically just ate everything and was as happy as could be! I would sit there (in silence, of course) and smile after every bite because I couldn't believe how delicious everything was! If you read my journal that week, you would have read a lot about me describing in great detail just how DELICIOUS every morsel was! I felt deep gratitude with each new food, and I felt like my cheeks hurt from all the smiling I did and the giddiness I felt.

It had been a long time since I had eaten many of those foods, and everything tasted especially wonderful with onions and garlic, two ingredients that I'd been restricted from for so long. (For anyone who has had to go without them for some time, you know what I'm talking about!) Even more FUN was eating dessert! I tasted the most delicious brownies I have ever eaten in my life, and I even had seconds. I then ate the leftover dessert the next day as a SNACK! I emphasize this part because I used to have all these silly rules around eating and meals and not snacking, so the fact that I was eating dessert (with SUGAR in it) as a snack was a big deal!

I hadn't planned on eating these foods that week, but the more I really heard myself, I felt love pulling me to try them and enjoy every moment and mouthful! It was also a chance to really listen to my body and test out eating for pleasure and enjoyment while desensitizing my body, nervous system, and digestive system's responses.

This fun only continued as the weeks went on.

Pizza was the biggest "reintroduction" of all the foods. Why? Not only does it deserve an award for being the best food, pizza is very high on the NO list! So, eating it was PURE FREEDOM. The melty cheese (dairy), the chewy crust (gluten), and the yummy sauce and toppings (more forbidden ingredients) combined to make every moment of eating it pure bliss! I think my happiness level canceled out all fear because it was SO. FUCKING. DELICIOUS!

The week before the retreat, I went to a friend's housewarming party that happened to be on Cinco de Mayo. If you know me, you know how much I have always loved a good theme party, especially one centered around guacamole and tequila! For years I had not been able to join in on this kind of evening. And though I still felt some resistance, I knew it was time . . . for the tequila and lime!

It was honestly the best night ever and brought so much healing and wholeness and FUN with my friends back into my life! What started off as a party with friends (something I had been unable to take part in for many years without feeling the many symptoms that would accompany it) led to a night of huge revelations. After eating lots and lots of guacamole (with onions and garlic included) and nachos, and drinking PLENTY of tequila and margaritas, my friends and I decided to go out dancing at a bar.

They were so excited that we could do this together since it wasn't something we had ever really been able to do in our friendship, so we enthusiastically hopped in an Uber and went downtown! The fact that I *could* do this was everything. The fact that I could *choose* where I wanted to be and feel safe in these places and moments was all I had wanted.

What happened that night shaped the rest of my life, knowing my belief and feeling could make any desired experience finally possible! And FUN!

We let the night guide us and ended up going to a bar called Locals Only. There was a sign outside it that read: "Join us or die." The truth is, in the past, joining in on this kind of outing kind of did feel like dying because I knew how awful I'd feel from the repercussions. I would have severe symptoms for days on end (even if I didn't have a drink). But this time was different.

I remember laughing and thinking, *Well I don't feel like dying today, so I guess we might as well join!* And join we did! I felt more alive that night than I had ever felt before. There was this feeling of FREEDOM, of limitless possibilities, that came from the ability to finally choose what I wanted in my life. I felt excited. I felt empowered. I felt magical!

We danced and sang the night away—until last call, I might add!

Goodbye 7:00 p.m. bedtime! So many of the songs that played were the same ones that I had listened to while doing my visualizations. It was like everything came full circle! This was the celebration of all the healing I had done prior to this moment, and it was the next step of healing for me.

In the past, going out would have been an opportunity to get my flirt on and look out for a man I might be interested in dating. But that night, I wasn't really interested, and I knew why.

I knew it was because I was just so happy to be in the moment, to be out with friends, and to be living life fully. I was fully in love with myself and the person I had grown into through this journey of finding my true self. I finally felt more ME than I ever had.

I remember the moment I had this realization.

I was dancing with a guy who was visibly perplexed by me and what vibe I was giving off. He didn't know what to do with me, so he asked, "What do you want?"

I loved that.

I loved everything about that question because it was in that question that I realized the answer: absolutely NOTHING.

I didn't want for anything because in that moment *I had everything I had ever wanted.* I had found who I was meant to be all along this wonky, wobbly healing journey, and I had found wholeness within myself. I was having FUN again and was finally getting to LIVE! I had also found love without needing to search for it outside of myself.

That is what life is all about. That is what we are all searching for, and all we have to do is search within. That's where the power lies—in our ability to love what is already there, to love what needs to be loved, and to live from that place of pure unconditional love, allowing whatever *is* to simply be as it *is*. Complete acceptance and love for it all.

These are the moments when instantaneous healing can happen. When we no longer feel like we need something outside of ourselves to be okay or feel good enough, miracles happen.

It's like the click when suddenly it all shifts after everything that has brought us to this moment.

It was the first time I no longer feared or really cared if I was perfectly healed. I was at peace with who and where I was in the moment, and this feeling of gratitude in the present was everything.

I was at peace with being perfectly imperfect in every way and realized that what I had wanted to feel was exactly the way I was feeling right then. The feelings of love, connection, and play that I had missed out on all those years were there, and I was finally joining in. In order to get there, I first had to go within.

TAKEAWAY & P L A Y
(BUT MOSTLY PLAY!)

Go within.

Hear yourself and what you need (but most importantly, what you truly WANT!).

Is it to play and finally JOIN IN, in your way? What do you need in order to start LIVING again?

What is it time to start doing, playing, and fully ENJOYING again?

This is the end. But more than anything, it's the beginning of the rest of your life.

And this time, it's actually yours. You have YOU back, and maybe it's the first time you have been this *you*. Maybe it's the first time you have truly seen who you were and are meant to be, what you are capable of, what your mind, body, and soul are capable of when embraced with love for all of YOU (including the sludgy mud!).

Maybe this is the first time you've had this much freedom because you finally allowed yourself to be led by the pull of your heart, your inner knowing, and trusted your body to lead

TAKEAWAY & P L A Y

you home to yourself! That is total freedom! Knowing that you will be okay, no matter what. Knowing that even though the road might feel long, sometimes muddy, filled with potholes, and other times scenic detours, the choice is yours. You have the choice to live a life that feels like YOU again.

So, take away whatever you choose to take from this book and LIVE AND LOVE YOUR LIFE.

It's YOUR life, nobody else's.

Remember that you get to choose. Every choice, every moment: it's yours now.

It's time for you to be YOU and do whatever your heart desires!

I believe your FEELINGS are guiding your way, so bake that cake.

Celebrate and eat it. Share it. Enjoy it. Not every moment will be cake-filled, but you will no longer fear the feelings or the things you used to be scared to enjoy; instead, you can be present and love whatever is here, right now. Be there for it all and have this

TAKEAWAY & P L A Y

recipe in your box—while still living outside the box—knowing you have you and your team by your side ready to play and learn alongside you.

Let yourself learn to get messy and magical!

Repeat. (And remix anytime you need . . . dance away and PLAY!)

Epilogue

A HEARTFELT, TRUTHFUL NOTE TO YOU

This is a truth-telling book, not a book about sugarcoating my journey, although I do reference cake a lot.

I want to tell you one last story. It's a heartwarming one. It will remind you that you don't have to get it perfect. You never did. It's the "Sparkle Story," and it's about the first time people started to notice that my health and well-being were improving. It is bigger than that, though. The truth of this moment would keep carrying me forward whenever I, or others, forgot. On this particular day I was visiting my mentor and dear friend and her daughter. During our time sitting, chatting, and catching up over tea, she looked at me and said, "Amanda, it's like you got your sparkle back." My mom had used those exact words too.

In that moment her daughter looked at her and said very loudly and matter-of-factly, "NO, MOM! Amanda never lost her sparkle, it was here the whole time!" She was pointing at my heart. I share this story here, knowing that the heart has got you from here on out.

You may be like her mom and think *you finally found it again* as you begin experiencing feeling better. But your heart, your sparkle, was and is always there just waiting for you to lean in, to love, to tap into its magic and make something beautiful out of any mud you encounter.

You get to have your HAPPY, and because this book is about truth-telling, I'm also going to give you the "human" ending, as the happiest endings are the ones that remind us that we get to be human too. And I will always take a stand for playing just as much as honoring and making friends with our emotions. If human-ing has felt tricky up to this point, we will navigate the next part together and break it down.

Remember, you get to use everything that feels honoring for you. You also get to keep looking for and allowing yourself to fully experience the rainbows that come after the storm (and mud).

I know that many people with a label or health challenge who have tried everything to get better can sometimes feel like they're hitting a wall. They may feel like NOTHING IS WORKING! Sometimes it's because we've been working too hard to heal, and other times it may be all that person knows. Somehow their whole identity has been linked to their illness. Getting better may be a fear for them that they don't realize is preventing them from having that miraculous "click moment."

Because illness has been such a big part of who they've felt they are for so long, it can feel scary to fully take it away and not be "that person" anymore but someone new altogether. I felt beyond grateful to not be the Amanda with a "brain injury" anymore, but at the same time, it was like starting life over again as a completely new person. After advocating for my challenges so I could get my needs met for so long, I now had to advocate for and remind people of my wellness.

I'm not going to lie, that part kind of sucked. It's enough to do everything to take yourself from sick and surviving to thriving and loving life without having to educate and remind people when they may not see this new truth.

This next part was a bit like being a toddler learning to walk again who had a whole new context for life, learning, and living. I wasn't the me I had been, and I also had a lot to learn, things to catch up on, and new dreams to create. It was almost as if now that I had "this cake," I was gathering the ingredients for a whole new cake—the next chapter of my life. That's the real truth. It's messier than the magic I shared in the last chapter, but it's so very REAL.

I think that's what my next chapter is about: being who I am and being okay with being human, being real, being messy, being imperfect, and LOVING with all that I received through this part.

Sometimes we feel like we hit a high and then we're "done." It's like in a really good song when the singer hits a HIGH NOTE, and it's almost like the song ends—that mic drop moment.

But if I left you there, you might expect the rest of your journey to simply be more of that (and only that!). You'll probably have mud again and you may experience unknowns and new experiences that are going to need ALL the learning from your journey, not just the last part!

So, I want to set you up for what's next. And, oh boy . . . do I wish someone would have done that for me!

The real integration happens when we keep repeating what aligns for us and expanding that feeling until it becomes our norm, our new way of being. We have to keep believing and recreating the steps that got us to where we are . . . while using them to help take us where we are choosing to go next.

So, what did I learn?

When it all feels dark and full of mud, pause, ask for help, pray or say what you need in some way. Make friends with your big feelings and emotions. Let yourself be guided: trust who and what shows up for you . . . face your fears and the things you really want again by doing it one next step and moment at a time. Face your fears with love. Ditch the fixing, your Ps and patterns; instead, pause, step back, and consciously choose to STAY AND PLAY! All this allows you to lean into your new way with compassion and while enjoying the present moment, trusting yourself fully. And FEELING all THE FEELS you want to feel while amplifying your high-vibe emotions to create new possibilities with the heart!

Remember, you get to celebrate your wins while minimizing your focus on the missteps (which in essence is rewriting your story and rewiring your brain). You get to start the next part with everything you learned through this journey. Reflecting on my personal journey helped me realize that humanness sometimes involves sharing the fears or missteps in order to receive the support we need. Then we can continue to celebrate our wins all over again!

And this is all part of how to reintegrate into the real world—post-lotus journey.

While writing, I knew that if I left some things out, this book wouldn't feel whole. And as I've mentioned throughout this book, **healing is about wholeness.** So, I'm leaving it all on the floor (and am then going to let you head to your own personal dance floor!).

Writing this book brought me to a place of even more wholeness within. I also want to stress that this journey doesn't end. The perfectionist pattern may not believe this fact, and yet the human journey means we are never "healed"—but we are always enough no matter where we are on our personal journey, which is why we get to live and enjoy life no matter what, rather than wait for "fixed," "healed," or "perfect" to start having fun. There is always some part in us that will desire well-rounded wholeness. But there is no need to go on a never-ending search or fix-it mission. Writing this book helped me remember this, and I also realized that after having had this journey, there were some missing steps that I had needed to learn while dancing it out myself. So, this book is all about supporting you as you go your own way too!

Some things happened after leaving my appointments, leaving the rulebook, and playing my way through every day. And before I share those things, I want you to know that my way is not *your* way. You don't need to leave all your appointments to heal or to find wholeness. It isn't about repeating the rules, steps, or my way.

It's about letting you be guided to yours, while letting me and my journey be that guide for you.

Only you know what's true for you.

So, back to what happened after that last chapter? A LOT happened and some old ways and patterns popped up a bit too. This is so very "human," but I also don't want you to make the same mistakes I did.

(Even though mistakes really are our first attempt in learning!)

Thus, I'd rather share it all so you can have a more integrated healing experience than the wonky, wobbly way I had. This is the recipe to healing, and I do believe in it wholeheartedly. I still use the steps today. I also believe in finding a middle way between "going your own way" and "we're all in this together."

That's the thing.

After having that "I have a NEW way moment," I lost my way a little. I got scared—scared to trust others and scared to be a patient again (or to be *vulnerable*). I got scared about telling it like it is and saying what is real and what I truly feel because I thought I had to only FEEL and focus on the HAPPY, the FUN, and the JOY. I feared that if I felt feelings that weren't positive that I'd get sick again.

I've learned a lot since then.

I realized that maybe my ability to fully feel emotions is true freedom. Feelings are what we create with our mind, but emotions are our response to an event that are asking to be fully felt, heard, and held so we don't hang onto them in our body until something shakes us up to finally let them go.

I learned that maybe if I felt safe within myself then all my emotions would feel safe too. But the thing about trauma is that we don't quite feel safe. We still feel like we need to be in control. And even finding our fun, focusing on *how* we want to feel, and all these empowering and incredible tools are still in control in a bit of a different way. At the same time, they can give us the power to take our own healing into our own hands.

But we don't need to be the only hands—we needn't forget to let others hold us too.

Remember how part of what I was missing in my life prior to finally surrendering and letting people in was actually letting others see ALL OF ME and hold me, even the parts that felt scared, broken, unlovable, and messy?

Once I "got better," I felt like I had to be perfect; I felt like I couldn't ever be sick again. And that's a big expectation to put on myself. I also felt like I was **so powerful** that everything that happened in my life was because of me, my thoughts, and my feelings, which is also a lot of pressure—pressure to feel only positive thoughts, feelings, and ALWAYS EXPECT THE BEST. But this doesn't allow the wholeness of life to seep in, which means that all feelings have a place, and that messiness and our humanness are lovable and welcome too.

It also didn't allow me to feel safe to fully be me with all the feelings and parts of me included. And it definitely didn't allow for me to feel safe to ask for help or to really receive it. And that is something we all need, and we need to feel safe when doing so. We need to be able to fall down and to get back up with other people holding us, helping us, and guiding us (even if we finally hear, trust, and guide ourselves too). I experienced a lot of not feeling like I could have this support, even after receiving so much already. I know how silly this may seem since learning to receive it was such a big lesson for me, but don't forget that there is no quota on how much love, support, acceptance, and guidance you are worthy of receiving from yourself or from others.

The way forward isn't doing it all on your own, it's trusting yourself while trusting others to hold you when you need it. Also, staying true to yourself, even if others don't agree.

For instance, I learned that sometimes when your "inner ding" speaks, you need to listen. Personally, I had a lot of post aha moments mentioned in this book when I was strongly guided to do something, like start my business, for example. The thought was scary, it made no logical sense, yet everything was ahead for me because I trusted it was.

I knew there was a lot I didn't know about being a business owner. My heart was clear that it was time and that my vision to take everything I learned from this full-heart healing and neuroplasticity-based experience to help others was needed in the world. I also knew there was more that I needed to learn too, which is why I continued to share my needs, ask for help, and learn.

This also meant sharing what I knew to be true and supporting the parents and children who were ready for the coaching and play-based support that I could help them with—to help find their own way moving forward while letting me hold them along the way, just as I had to let my "team" do for me. And doing so has allowed me to help parents and children feel like themselves again, find their fun, make friends with their feelings, and be their true selves. We start at the root, the heart, and the heart of it all: seeking wholeness, healing, and fun for the whole family, one session, one big emotion, one dance party, one breathwork session, or one sing-along song at a time. By both being and doing. By working the steps in this book. By taking that action (facing one fear at a time) while playing, learning, and making friends with my own emotions with my intuition guiding me one day, one aligned action step, and one client at a time. It all came full circle.

Speaking of circles, I recently had a friend tell me a story about circle time. I'm not talking about the circle time you may have had at school. It's more like a prayer circle where all people come as equals. They learn together, they share together, and nobody knows more than another: everyone is vulnerable, open, and willing to learn something new.

That is what this chapter is reminding you.

"Take what you take and leave what you leave." –Jenn Walker

This advice from a fellow coach was something I needed to learn. I could still hold my beliefs while expanding them while seeing others as helping me to do so. And I badly needed to hear it and learn from it at the time, so I could expand my mind as well as my heart's ability to connect with others and fully let them in.

Know that your "knowing" means you have a deepened awareness and trust in yourself. But it doesn't mean that other people are wrong, that their way isn't also a "new way" that can help you, or that in order to "stay well," you have to do the opposite of what you did before. This isn't about extremes, rights or wrongs, or doing the opposite of what you used to do. Just like the yin and yang, we have all parts within us, and that's where balance comes in.

It's not about perfection or doing any of the steps perfectly. It's about listening when some things are "not quite balanced" and need a little more love and nurturing.

We don't need the rules, *we need each other*.

And what my friend shared about circle time is that **showing up is the most important part.**

Sometimes you are the teacher when you come to the circle. Sometimes you are the learner. There are days when you need the circle, and there are days when the circle needs you. **Don't be afraid to learn from others while staying true to yourself.**

And listen to your gut while staying curious.

There is always more to learn. There is always more to teach. And like in the "healing partnership," we can do, grow, learn, and experience more when we share in it together.

Doing it alone keeps you alone.

Simply put, trauma is a loss of connection. Although I felt better in many ways, I still didn't know how to feel a connection with others because I had felt *so alone* for so long—so separate. I think that's what a lot of we humans feel sometimes—we feel like we are the only ones experiencing whatever it is we're suffering from. **The truth is, though, that we are not alone, and we are definitely not the only ones.**

Just like how nobody saw when I was sick because my brain injury was invisible, it was hard for others to see that I was healthy and fully able to join in once I could. I was unsure of how to navigate this part while staying in my "new" because I often felt that people saw me as I once was. The essence of me was (and is) still the same, and yet so much had changed. And I had to remind myself that although I know I had evolved, as did the key support system who was there with me on this journey, there would always be people who couldn't quite reconcile the person I used to be with the person I am still becoming every single day.

Some people will hang on to the version of you (and connect or relate with you) in a way that makes the most sense for them to do so. This is *their* limitation, their way of seeing things, and perhaps their humanness too. And I could choose whether to take those ways of seeing me as my truth. My only priority was to be me and to do my best to live a life that was grounded in love for myself, in kindness for myself and my body, and in compassion for both myself and the other people around me.

It took me a while to fully integrate who I was rather than who I felt like I needed to be to stay healthy. I didn't need to ditch ALL the parts of me that I felt got me sick, thus becoming an opposite version of what I was. **I just needed to feel safe being me.** And part of that meant learning to let others in again in very vulnerable ways. Part of that meant having others hold me as I learned to feel again.

I have learned a lot about healing from trauma; and sometimes, when we finally see a light at the end of the tunnel, we hang on for dear life to the way or the thing that got us better. We control so we can stay well, which isn't truly wholeness.

My real freedom came from really learning that it was safe to BE ME. That is, knowing that all my feelings are safe—to know, to hear, to feel, to listen, and to express. That part wasn't as easy as baking a cake by following the steps of a recipe. But that's the real truth. And I honestly believe we are learning and practicing this lesson every single day.

Let the steps guide you. Also, please know that baking a fake cake isn't the point. You want to fully embrace and enjoy the cake-baking process, even if the cake doesn't rise every time. Sometimes the beauty in and best part of making a cake is that you can make a mess and totally giggle and have FUN doing it! And while you're having fun trying to bake and create the yummiest cake (which in essence is your life, your health, and your "soul map" back home to you), you find magic in those moments when your recipe goes sideways and your cake doesn't taste or look the way you imagined. The key is to have fun, experiment, play, enjoy the mess, and ultimately find your own special blend of cake mix to bake and decorate—because that special blend is YOU.

Don't be too scared to mess up because messing up can be a fun and teachable moment when we allow it to be.

As Ms. Frizzle in *The Magic School Bus* says, "Take chances. Make mistakes. GET MESSY!"

Embracing the mess is also your message. So let the mess bring meaning and make you MORE YOU.

Ask for what you need rather than controlling every single thing.

Say how you really feel. Know that your feelings are a powerful and empowering tool. Keep visualizing while staying open to the fact that things may go differently than you planned. Keep believing while remembering that there are others holding on to that feeling with you (but only if you let them in, learn to trust again, and let them hold you in your big vision). This is the real recipe. Welcome the mess, the mud, and all of it.

Because there is no real rulebook to life or your own healing journey. **You are your own guide.** And part of life is letting others be there for the ride, joining in alongside you, and learning together, laughing together, and figuring it out together.

You need partners on that dance floor. We are never meant to dance alone.

If you need some help along your journey, please get in touch. I would be honored to let my learning support you in yours. And remember that when you get stuck, that's what we have each other for. Don't be afraid to reach out for the support and guidance you're worthy of receiving.

And if it hadn't been for me asking for more, for leaning on others once again, I wouldn't have been able to write this book. I wouldn't have been able to embody the ability to embrace the messiness and beautiful person that is ME who is still always learning, playing, loving, and accepting every single day.

And remember, if you get stuck, if the mud gets BIG, use the tools, and mostly PAUSE, play, ask for help, and let yourself be guided to *your* way.

Your way is to stay in the faith.

Stay in the belief and hope.

And know that no matter what, you are you, and that is *indeed* enough.

THE FINAL

TAKEAWAY & P L A Y

This is where you integrate. This is where the "click moments" get to keep happening for you! This is the moment when you really lean into trusting yourself and what feels aligned for you.

I want you to take some time to honor you and your journey.

Remember all you have read, learned, practiced, and tried!

- What worked for you?
- What felt honoring?
- What shifted things for you?
- How can you keep repeating it and coming back to it (when you need it, as well as repeatedly and consistently) as something you KNOW feels supportive? Like PLAY, making friends with those big emotions, asking for help, and saying what you need! Praying and making way for a new way, even if you don't know what that might be. Allow yourself to be reminded of the lessons here. And of the people who helped you learn them.

The ones that taught you something new, the things that made you feel most like YOU.

TAKEAWAY & P L A Y

And remember who you are. Because although you have come so far, you may still need some reminders if you forget. Life is a continuous journey. It's not a race to the finish line—because we will never get there. We are always evolving, growing, and learning, which means that you will still need tools, love, acceptance, connection, and ways to support you and your life.

So now that you're living again, how will you choose to live? What are the ingredients for your best life?

What do you need to prioritize? What do you want to add in? Or release? What do you need to be reconnected to? What do you need to be reminded of that is a pattern and not actually you?

What are your biggest takeaways from this *Eat PLAY Love* journey?

I would love to know! Do it for you, and if you wish to share (because sharing IS always caring), please send me an email at amanda@mindbodysoulmiracles.com. What touched your heart? What were your big SHIFTS or aha moments? What are you taking away? How has your life changed by reading this book? I want to know what you overcame, what you left in the

TAKEAWAY & P L A Y

past, and how your life is now while you are starting anew. You may need someone to cheer you on and "see you" in this next part, and I would LOVE to see you and the wins!

And in the words of my publishing house: You got this! (I know you do). I trust you. You made it this far, and I know how much you have been through. Just like the Shania Twain song, it's all up from here! Savor and revel in the moments you feel like celebrating. And in the moments you feel down, may you always be reminded that these rock bottom, sludgy, muddy moments are what lead you up, Up, UP—to full bloom like the beautiful lotus! Dance it out, shake it out, and just celebrate who you are, where you've been, and how far you have come! Seriously, go do a happy dance! So, in completion, can you DANCE?

Your last PLAY is to listen to the song that brings you to your happiest, healthiest, most alive and aligned "I FUCKING DID IT!" celebration. Dance your heart out! This last one is just for you!

With love and gratitude,

Amanda

Resources

BOOKS

Becoming Supernatural: How Common People Are Doing the Uncommon by Dr. Joe Dispenza, 2014, Hay House

Breaking the Habit of Being Yourself by Dr. Joe Dispenza, 2019, Hay House

Days of Grace: A Memoir by Arthur Ashe and Arnold Rampersad, 1993, Knopf

Love, Medicine and Miracles by Bernie Siegel, 1999, Rider

Option B: Facing Adversity, Building Resilience, and Finding Joy by Sheryl Sandberg, 2019, WH Allen

Self-Compassion: The Proven Power of Being Kind to Yourself by Kristin Neff, 2011, Yellow Kite

Stress Less, Accomplish More: Meditation for Extraordinary Performance by Emily Fletcher, 2020, William Morrow & Company

The Brain's Way of Healing by Dr. Norman Doidge, 2016, Penguin

The Connected Child by Dr. Karyn B. Purvis, 2007, McGraw-Hill Education

The 5 Personality Patterns: Your Guide to Understanding Yourself and Others and Developing Emotional Maturity by Steven Kessler, 2021, Bodhi Free Press

The Gifts of Imperfection by Brené Brown, 2020, Penguin

The Power of Now by Eckhart Tolle, 2001, Generic

The Universe Has Your Back: Transform Fear to Faith by Gabrielle Bernstein, 2016, Hay House

Untethered Soul by Michael A. Singer, 2020, Sounds True

We're Going on a Bear Hunt by Michael Rosen, 1993, Walker Books

You Can Heal Your Life by Louise Hay, 1984, Hay House

You Are the Placebo: Making Your Mind Matter by Dr. Joe Dispenza, 2014, Hay House

INSPIRING QUOTES

Meister Eckhart

Albert Einstein

Audrey Hepburn

Reinhold Niebuhr

Rumi

Siddhartha Guatama Shakyamuni

Jenn Walker (https://diveheartfirst.com/)

Lemony Snicket

MOVIES

Eat Pray Love (Ryan Murphy, director, 2010, Sony Pictures Entertainment)

Mean Girls (Mark Waters, director, 2004, Paramount Pictures)

TV

Grey's Anatomy (2005–present, Disney ABC Television)

The Magic School Bus (1994–1997, Scholastic)

SONGS

"Bet On It" written by Antonina Armato and Tim James, performed by Zac Efron, 2007

"Breaking Free" written by Jamie Houston, performed by Zac Efron and Vanessa Hudgens, 2006

"Don't Stop Believin'" written by Journey (Jonathan Cain, Steve Perry, Neal Schon), performed by Journey, 1981

"Gotta Catch 'Em All" written by John Siegler and John Loeffler, performed by Jason Paige, 1999

"Gotta Go My Own Way" written by Andy Dodd and Adam Watts, performed by Zac Efron and Vanessa Hudgens, 2007

"My Favorite Things" written by Oscar Hammerstein and Richard Rodgers, performed by Julie Andrews, 1959

"We're All in This Together" written by Matthew Gerrard and Robbie Nevil, performed by Zac Efron, Vanessa Hudgens, Lucas Grabeel, Ashley Tisdale, 2008

"Start of Something New" written by Matthew Gerrard and Robbie Nevil, performed by Zac Efron, Drew Seeley, and Vanessa Hudgens, 2006

MEDITATION

Calm

Eat PLAY Love meditation (www.mindbodysoulmiracles.com/eat-play-love)

Gabby Bernstein meditation (gabbybernstein.com)

Headspace

Insight Timer

HEALING PROGRAMS

HeartMath Institute (www.heartmath.org)

HeartMath Institute empowers individuals, families, groups, and organizations to enhance their life experiences using tools that enable them to better recognize and access their intuitive insight and heart intelligence.

Elementum Coaching Institute (www.elementumcoachinginstitute.com)

A Nine-Month Training where you will learn and embody the skills to be a master coach.

Mind Body Soul Miracles (www.mindbodysoulmiracles.com/eat-play-love)

A safe space for families to heal together through love, connection, and PLAY.

Acknowledgments

To all who helped me on my healing path, my heart is forever grateful. To all who saw me when I couldn't see myself, thank you.

To my mom and dad, thanks for loving me. I could not have made it through without you, your support, and all the ways you helped me find and access what I needed (and thanks for embracing the "play way" and for being willing to join me in kitchen dance parties!).

To my sister, Allie, and my sister from another mister, Geneva, thanks for all the ways you were both there through the hardest years. For the laughs, the presence, the listening, the joy you brought in the simplest of moments, and for simply "being there." I couldn't have done it without you, and I know that must not have always been easy for each of you. And yet, you were there.

To the many practitioners, coaches, healers, and helpers on my expansive "team." I am forever grateful for the way you held space, for never giving up on me or on what was possible for me. Thanks for being an extended family when I needed it and thanks to all the families near and dear to my heart that let me be in theirs. You know who you are, and I can't thank you enough for the countless generous offers to learn with you, from you, as well as from your children.

Thanks to the many kiddos who helped me find my sparkle again! And for reminding me of what truly matters. And a big thank you to anyone who helped me have somewhere to sleep and stay while navigating my (what seemed like endless) appointments and back-and-forth trips.

To anyone who shared their own journey with me or held space for me, thank you. I can't thank you enough and know there are too many people for me to ever try to name.

Thank you to everyone on the YGTMedia Publishing Team who helped birth this book baby.

And thanks for the nudge from the Universe that came when it was time to get the book finished, and to Maddie for sitting with me in Gibson and Co.'s coffee shop in Collingwood, writing, editing, and chatting with me in the early stages of the book-writing process. Thanks for your listening ear and heart and helping me get the ball rolling when I had left the book for a bit.

Thanks to every song and every coffee shop that made this book possible. I don't know what I would have done without the many sound-tracks of fun and coffees that made this book happen!

Last but not least, a big heartful thanks to Winston (my puppy who came along during this book-writing journey) and Sam. Thank you for simply "being" with me: for your joyful presence, silliness, and fun you both added to my life—especially during the birthing of this book. Thanks for being the reminders of the importance of "staying and play-ing," pausing to appreciate the little moments and for always being game to play the "What Makes Me Happy" game with me. And being part of what makes me happy!

Thanks to the magic of this book for reminding me of what I needed to keep practicing and living.

Thank you, reader, for being my why. I watched a movie the weekend we were finishing editing on this book and there was a big line in it that stayed with my heart.

The main character (a dancer) was asked why she danced. The why was what set her apart.

And I always come back to: Why do I write? It's for you. And also for me. So, from my big, sparkly, loving (full of superpowers) HEART to yours, thank you!

Author Bio

Amanda Evans is a family play-based healer, author, and master coach (meets Mary Poppins!). She is passionate about supporting children and families to be their happiest and healthiest selves. Her own healing journey taught her so much about the extraordinary healing powers of love, connection, and play! She is dedicated to helping people take their health and happiness into their own hands by believing in their own magic and the power to heal from within. Amanda coaches conscious parents who are triggered by their child's tantrums, big emotions, and disempowering diagnoses to parent with greater ease, connection, presence, and PLAY! Amanda is a dog mama and a lover of little humans and the little moments (that really are the BIG ones!).

 mind_body_soul_miracles

www.mindbodysoulmiracles.com

YGTMedia Co. is a blended boutique publishing house for mission-driven humans. We help seasoned and emerging authors "birth their brain babies" through a supportive and collaborative approach. Specializing in narrative nonfiction and adult and children's empowerment books, we believe that words can change the world, and we intend to do so one book at a time.

ygtmedia.co/publishing

@ygtmedia.company

@ygtmedia.co

www.ingramcontent.com/pod-product-compliance
Lightning Source LLC
Chambersburg PA
CBHW061143120626
46546CB00005B/1910